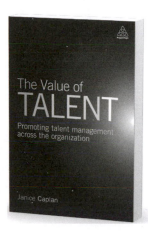

The Value
of Talent

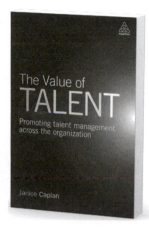

The Value of Talent

Promoting talent management across the organization

Janice Caplan

KoganPage

LONDON PHILADELPHIA NEW DELHI

First published in Great Britain and the United States in 2011 by Kogan Page Limited

120 Pentonville Road
London N1 9JN
United Kingdom
www.koganpage.com

525 South 4th Street, #241
Philadelphia PA 19147
USA

4737/23 Ansari Road
Daryaganj
New Delhi 110002
India

© Janice Caplan, 2011

The right of Janice Caplan to be identified as the author of this work has been asserted by her in accordance with the Copyright, Designs and Patents Act 1988.

ISBN   978 0 7494 5984 0
E-ISBN   978 0 7494 5985 7

British Library Cataloguing-in-Publication Data

A CIP record for this book is available from the British Library.

Library of Congress Cataloging-in-Publication Data

Caplan, Janice.
    The value of talent : aligning personal development with organizational success / Janice Caplan.
        p. cm.
    Includes bibliographical references.
    ISBN 978-0-7494-5984-0 – ISBN 978-0-7494-5985-7   1. Manpower planning.   2. Personnel management.   3. Human capital–Management.   I. Title.
    HF5549.5.M3C36 2010
    658.3'14–dc22
                                                                                            2010028707

Typeset by Graphicraft Limited, Hong Kong
Printed and bound in India by Replika Press Pvt Ltd

CONTENTS

PREFACE

The value of talent: promoting talent management across the organization

The aim of this book is not just to add to the debate on talent management but also to provide HR practitioners and business leaders with sound practical advice for workable and innovative solutions. Many of my ideas represent new ways of doing things; many others have been done before. However, when all of them are taken together, I believe they amount to a new approach to managing people and organizations that suits our times and that is essential for long-term business survival in a rapidly changing world.

The ideas in this book have been developed from my practical experience and from extensive research and reading. Most of the current writing on talent management still focuses on 'identifying, developing and promoting your best people'. While much of it offers excellent models and processes, the notion of an approach that focuses on 'your best people' is limited. As you develop this line of thinking, it runs up against all sorts of hurdles, not least of which is the difficulty of identifying what makes someone a 'best' person in today's fast-moving working environment, where many roles are becoming increasingly interconnected – and where junior roles may actually turn out to be pivotal. Moreover, as organizations become ever leaner, every person becomes yet more important to their organization's success.

I have sought to develop a holistic approach that more than anything is based on sound common sense and that also makes life easier for line managers on whom the responsibility for putting talent management into practice generally falls.

My working experience, over the past few years in particular, has given me a privileged opportunity to develop and apply the ideas and thinking that have led to this book. There are three strands to this:

- One strand has been my consultancy work with leading businesses and business people, which has given me the chance to develop and prove new programmes and ideas. I have also had to step into the breach to make up for staff shortages at senior level, reminding me of corporate life at the sharp end. Other assignments have given me a first-hand perspective of the challenges facing people at the top, combined with a close involvement in day-to-day operations and the demands made of people on the ground.

- Another strand to the experience that informs this book has been my role as a vice-president of the CIPD (Chartered Institute of Personnel and Development). This has enabled me to work with and learn from the CIPD's own knowledgeable and talented research teams, as well as leading HR directors, practitioners and academics. It has brought me into contact with the HR and business practices of countless organizations, giving me an overview of what is going on in the profession. Conversations with peers have been invaluable in helping me hone my ideas and thinking.

- The third strand to my work experience over the last decade has been my partnering with ACE European HR consortium. This has enabled me to work with an international, multicultural and sometimes virtual team; this is the epitome of the experience of so many businesses in a globalized world and has added to the depth and breadth of my outlook. It has also given me direct, first-hand experience of steering a business through the different phases of its development.

In all my work, I have had the support and contribution of my outstanding business partner of many years, Carolyn Ponder, who has had a significant role in helping me develop my thinking and my professionalism. Carolyn and I have had a truly exceptional, and also immensely enjoyable, business career together. More recently, I have had the privilege of learning and benefiting from the support of my other colleagues in Scala and in ACE.

ACKNOWLEDGEMENTS

Many organizations and individuals have been exceptionally generous with their time, experience and insights in helping me write this book. My family have been extremely supportive and my husband, *Brian Finch*, reviewed my writing and helped me think through many ideas.

I have a special debt of gratitude to: *David Reay*, global talent and HR capability lead, BAE Systems, who was enormously generous with his time and effort, reading, rereading, reviewing and commenting on all chapters of this book. I have benefited greatly from his incisive feedback and insightful comments.

My appreciation also to *Mike Crimes* of The Scala Group and ACE, *Clara Lodo* of IdeaManagement and ACE, *Andrew Menhennet* of AM Reward Consulting, and *Daniel Ephraty* for reading and commenting on chapters of this book and offering advice.

This book also benefits from the detailed case studies and observations that have been given to me by:

Tim Miller, director, property, research and assurance, Standard Chartered, and chairman, Standard Chartered Korea; *Geraldine Haley*, group head, leadership effectiveness and succession, Standard Chartered; *Emma M Crosby*, leadership succession manager, Standard Chartered; *Veronica Munro*, leadership effectiveness facilitator, Standard Chartered; *Paul Herrick*, human resources managing director, EMEA, Burson Marsteller; *Neil Purshouse*, global HR manager, wire, Bekaert; *Carlin Deseyne*, CPM; *Carolyn Gray*, group HR director, Guardian Media Group; *Alison Hall*, head of change management, Guardian News and Media; *Fiona M Anderson*, editor, coaching, BBC College of Journalism, BBC; *Tony Worgan*, managing editor, Radio Wiltshire (on attachment to College of Journalism, BBC); *Sara Beck*, BBC journalism group; *Jodie King*, head of talent management, KPMG LLP; *David Fairhurst*, senior vice-president, chief people officer, McDonald's; *Jenny Arwas MBE*, HR director, BT Group Functions, BT; *Sam Austin-May*, deputy head of HR, European Southern Observatory; *Gwynne Hamlen*, vice-president, human resources, EMEA, ConvaTec.

Similarly, this book benefits from the specialist help and advice given by: *Michael Rose*, Rewards Consulting; *John McGurk*, CIPD adviser on learning and talent development.

Colin Rosen of The Scala Group and ACE, and *Martyn Sloman*, visiting professor at Kingston Business School, Kingston University, have been a constant guide and inspiration to me.

I would also like to pay tribute to the late *John Bailey*, director of coaching, KPMG LLP, whose help and advice were invaluable to me when I wrote *Coaching for the Future*. I have used his work and his notes to inform some of the thinking in this book.

Finally, *Hannah Berry*, my editor at Kogan Page, has been immensely patient and supportive and a pleasure to work with.

This new world

Everyone is important. Make talent important for everyone.
The central theme of this book is that the demands of a changed world are driving the evolution of talent management from being a strategy that deals with skills shortages and hiring new talent to a much more comprehensive one where it is a way of thinking and a way of doing things that aligns individual development with the needs and objectives of the organization. The ultimate aim of talent management is to create a high-performing organization that survives and prospers in a business environment that is undergoing unprecedented structural change.

The main characteristic of this structural change, common to all organizations, is the breathtaking speed with which change is happening. This speed is creating a new world organization where, more than ever before, everyone is important to the organization, where talent is important and where it is imperative to make talent important to everyone.

This chapter looks at the nature of the changes taking place and what this means to the organization. It also outlines the approach to talent management which is developed in the ensuing chapters.

How has talent management evolved?

Talent management has been high on the HR agenda for the past few years. It started in 1997, through McKinsey's 'War for Talent' study,[1] which identified recruitment as the number-one concern for business leaders. The problems were particularly acute because of skills shortages at senior management levels and so, at first, talent strategies were largely directed to improving recruitment at that level. But of course, the best way to overcome labour shortages, especially the global shortage of effective leaders, is to develop your own and retain them longer. And so the term 'talent management' began to grow to encompass assessing, developing and deploying people. As it did so there has been considerable debate about whether an organization should have an inclusive or an exclusive approach to talent. Does it cover everyone, or, as the Chartered Institute of Personnel and Development's working definition suggests, should it focus on 'those individuals with high potential who are of particular value to an organization'?[2] Those who favour an exclusive approach generally argue that talented performers are the individuals who are always going to have opportunities elsewhere; or that businesses should focus investment on the people who perform business-critical roles; or that businesses must know who their high performers and high potentials are so as to make extra efforts to retain them. Those who favour an inclusive approach often have different forms of inclusivity. Some organizations see inclusivity merely as involving additional groups, such as professional staff or technical experts, as well as those identified as having leadership potential. This may ignore the talent management of other groups of workers.

An added problem is that, as talent management has evolved, it has become a hotchpotch of ideas, practices and definitions; these lack coherence and focus, with the risk that talent management is more about trying to label disparate practices than it is about driving business performance. As the Institute of Employment Studies has pointed out, talent management has now evolved to the point where it 'describes a wide range of organizational practice, and the parts of the workforce to whom the term "talent" might apply can range from small numbers of potential senior leaders to everyone'.[3] They also argue that the HR profession has extended the core ideas of attracting and developing talent into every '–ing' you can think of: retaining, motivating, rewarding, etc. So at one extreme, talent management is the whole of the HR field and at the other it is only a new way of talking about future leaders.

Why talent management?

Does this matter? Yes, it does matter. The key argument of this book is that there is something really important here. Talent management can describe a different way of doing things that can be an immensely powerful idea, but using the term as a catch-all phrase dilutes its impact and its potential. Two terms that we commonly use, 'labour' and 'human capital,' are mechanistic terms that treat people as a commodity – but 'talent' implies people as individuals. To borrow from Shakespeare: 'What's in a name? That which we call a rose by any other name would smell as sweet.' So there is little point in using the term 'talent management' in a new way just to say the same thing. The usage described in this book truly is a different way of doing things.

Let us stand back for one moment and consider the context of the business environment that presents us with an exceptional set of circumstances representing an exceptional paradigm shift – something that is often written about but is usually an exaggeration; but not in this case.

What is the business case?

Today's business environment is characterized by global competition from the new economies such as China, India and Brazil and technologically driven structural change, as well as cyclical economic change. What makes this historically different is the breathtaking speed with which technology is changing the way we live, the way we do things and perhaps even the way we think.

It is possible to argue, of course, that this has happened before with the Industrial Revolution and also that the succession of new technologies in the Industrial Revolution, such as steam engines, mechanical engineering and materials technology, enabled each other just as now computing, communications, biotechnology and nanotechnology all reinforce and support development in each other. The latter two, for example, would not have occurred without development of and dramatic improvement in computing power, while the need for massive computer power to solve technological problems, such as gene sequencing, has stimulated the development of that power (even if the consumer demand for ever more sophisticated computer games has also had an influence). The huge difference between the industrial and knowledge revolutions is not just in the massive social and educational changes that have taken place in the meantime, but critically in the speed of change, which requires a different way of organizing and a different kind of individual response.

How is the speed of change so different and how can we visualize its acceleration? Think about that sophisticated but everyday device now used by millions of people around the globe, the Apple iPhone, and how we got to it in 2007. It took over 200 years from the early experiments with electricity before the transistor was developed in 1948. Then in just the next 40 years or so, all in a rush, we got serious computing, personal computers and hand-held devices. The worldwide web arrived at the end of that time. In the incredibly short time since then, commerce over the web has exploded from nothing to an estimated $204 billion in the USA alone in 2008. In 1998 Google reported 26 million web pages on its index; by 2000 it had one billion and by 2008 one trillion.[4] After less than 20 years, it is hard to imagine life without the web, available to us worldwide and now on tiny hand-held devices. The computer data centres that power the web now account for more than 1 per cent of world electricity production. Very soon web-enabled devices will be found in refrigerators and cookers. These changes over just 20 years have already fundamentally changed the way we do things.

Consider the effects of these changes on commerce: a fundamental change in the way books and music are distributed, possibly the eventual demise of the printed book, probably a change in the way news and opinion are delivered, the displacement of 'distributors', replaced by selling direct from producer to customer. Consider that the web has enabled e-mailing and social networking, as well as open-source problem solving. Among other effects this is reducing national mail services around the world at the same time as it increases parcel deliveries. The number of local post offices is dwindling, which affects social relations, and new systems have to be invented to provide the local services they used to. In saying that the world is different, one must also use the word 'globalization'. While international trade is not new and events in India affected Europe more than 200 years ago, the sheer scale and immediacy are different. Today a call centre servicing Europe or America can be in India or the Philippines or Kenya and, at the flip of a switch, can be somewhere else. Going back to that iPhone for illustration, parts for it were developed and manufactured in the USA and Europe and the Far East.

The speed of change has not levelled off and the business implications of the digital revolution, cheap broadband communications and the worldwide web have clearly not run their course. Even as computer speeds approach their theoretical limits, new technologies such as quantum computing may provide a further boost, which may enable us to do things we only dream of today. If and when this electronic revolution begins to slow, will there be a next big thing to maintain the speed of change? The foundations could be in the course of being laid for new biological technologies – and then after that...? The point is that new technologies do not just boost economic growth but have profound implications for what we do, how we do it and how we organize ourselves to do it.

Sometimes a sense of history helps us make sense of where we are now, so looking back at the HR landscape might be helpful. In the 1980s and 90s many businesses faced radical overhauls: great British institutions such as British Airways, British Gas, British Telecom and British Rail were privatized; television franchises were allocated; the telecommunications market was opened to competition; the financial markets were deregulated. In almost all these cases, these were structural changes that were signalled some time in advance and could, therefore, be prepared for by the organizations affected. Managing change and the knowledge economy were two of the hot topics in management thinking. We were at the start of the new information era and the digital revolution. State monopolies were being dismantled and having to face increasing competition and globalization. The cost of employing people had risen to levels where it became imperative to demand ever more from fewer people. 'Change' was something different and special because of the speed with which it was happening and we weren't used to that. To paraphrase Bill Gates, we also weren't used to managing assets that every evening went down in the lift and walked out of the building, and you could never be sure they would come back the next day. We responded to these challenges with ideas about flatter hierarchies, matrix structures of management, the learning organization and so on. So that by now an awareness of managing change and leading and managing knowledge and knowledge workers should be part of the fabric of most organizations. However, rather like a computer game, having mastered one level it is straight on to the next! What is different today, compared with yesterday and earlier times such as the Industrial Revolution, is that the speed of change today carries with it an unprecedented level of ambiguity and of uncertainty. It is hard to be certain of what will be the right or best business model for many industries and organizations in the next few years. What is certain is the need for learning, adapting, innovating and creating.

It is being widely commented by academics, intellectuals and business people that developed Western economies are moving from the knowledge or information economy to what is sometimes called the innovation economy or creative economy or the advanced knowledge economy. According to interviews conducted by the executive search firm Spencer Stuart, more than two-thirds of directors at the leading global companies it advises cite innovation as critical for long-term success.[5] That is not surprising given the environment described above. Rapid and often unpredictable change demands rapid reaction and an ability to anticipate it with new products and services: with innovation. Today's business environment requires people who can innovate, work across organizational boundaries and in partnerships, and who are sufficiently far-sighted and quick-sighted to spot trends, create opportunities and rapidly take advantage of these. Even in uncertainty, there are some things that will be clear, and there are some things that will remain the same. There are also some things that will present themselves as different options. It is about positioning the business so that when the right option becomes clear, the right people with the right skills are able to pursue it rapidly. If you can jump on a bandwagon, you may already be too late.

For individuals the result of all this will be a need to continually reappraise their skills, acquire new ones and also be flexible and fleet of foot. They need to have an eye on the horizon to spot changes as they emerge. They need to be able to create opportunities before others do. They need to be innovative, creative and adaptable and eagerly willing to learn. What impact will the increasing use of wikis (websites that allow anyone to create or edit pages) and open-source problem solving have on what I do? How will people's use of Twitter or Facebook, blogs or YouTube affect how I do my job? How can I take advantage of these developments? To quote Gary Hamel, businesses will have to 'find ways to get our employees to bring their creativity and their passion to work every day'.[6]

As we have already seen, exclusive approaches to talent management that focus on 'people of particular value' often miss the point; structural, rapid and unpredictable change means that today's business-critical role might be obsolete tomorrow and vice versa. The financial sector is an example of this: risk management skills that were sidetracked yesterday may be pivotal tomorrow. None of which should encourage a shrug and inaction: it is an argument for building resilience and flexibility into our organizations. It is also an argument for constantly reviewing business strategies, developing people policies that support those strategies and for actively managing the skills and capabilities throughout the organization to ensure that the right ones will be in place to achieve business goals and strategies: talent management.

Not all change is unpredictable. Focusing on what's on the horizon, whilst at the same time facilitating rapid response to change, is a major aim of talent management. A clear talent management strategy will enable us to identify where both the organization and individuals are now in terms of skills and capabilities, where they aspire and need to be, and will focus on actions to get from one to the other. It will not just recognise that people must be able to continually learn and adapt – that is a start and is where many organizations are already. The difference is that the talent management approach also engages people with the strategic outlook of the business and encourages people to develop capabilities that will be needed in the longer term. This is not just keeping up with the pace of change but keeping ahead of it.

This is a holistic approach that recognizes that in today's lean organization there is nowhere to hide for the merely adequate; and everyone matters. This approach, of course, includes special provision for exceptional performers and future leaders and also deals with underachievers and underperformers. It ensures that those who have reached their potential continually refresh their skills. It is likely to also include, or at least take into consideration, people who are not directly employed by you: contractors, suppliers, consultants, outsourced employees, or members of the public. One of the characteristics of the 'new economy' seems to be an increase in collaborative arrangements. This phenomenon takes different forms, from working with joint-venture partners, to collaborating with people you may never meet. This example is well illustrated by the development of the iPhone. One of the key factors in its success has been the mini applications or apps that Apple has enabled, earns a return from and authorizes but which are provided by a host of external collaborators.

The talent management approach empowers people to learn from job experiences and emphasizes the importance of providing people with stretching and developmental work. It challenges the people at the top of the organization to think through their strategies and the people they have and the capabilities that they need to deliver these strategies. In the 'new organization' innovation may not emanate from the top strategic level. Significant change, although shaped by the strategic vision coming from the leaders of the organization, may emerge in a team or an individual at any level. The inspiration or the insight for a new product or a new market or a new way of doing things may come from anyone. As Ed Lawler advocates, it also encourages an upstream approach where decisions about which business strategy to pursue are shaped by an understanding of the people who will make it happen.[7]

What does success look like?

In summary, today's nimble, flexible, innovative organization requires a talent management strategy that is about developing everyone's strengths, valuing diversity and encouraging creativity and innovation. It is about helping people achieve their aspirations through aligning individual and organizational development and minding the gap between organizational capability now and what will be required in the foreseeable future. This covers managing organizational capabilities, individual development, performance enhancement, leadership development, succession planning and workforce planning. It links with all parts of the HR agenda, especially recruitment, reward and employee engagement and is seamlessly integrated with business strategy. It is future focused, seeking to spot what is on the horizon and align organizational and individual development to this. It aims to keep the organization learning faster than the environment around it.

Talent management is not just about systems and processes but what you do with these and how you implement them so that you achieve a talent mindset across the organization. A talent mindset means that line managers will recognize their responsibility to manage talent effectively, just as they are expected to manage other resources. Directors or chief executives will review talent as critically as they review the organization's finances. Individuals will actively seek to develop or update their own talents. Individuals will be provided with the kind of developmental work experiences that build the organization's key capabilities. The HR function will enable this talent approach by crafting business-relevant talent management systems and processes and implementing them in a way that consistently reinforces the organization's values.

In today's business context, everyone is important, so make talent important for everyone.

My aim is for this book to be a guide for business leaders and HR practitioners on how to achieve outstanding talent management so as to retain flexibility and build long-term success in an uncertain world. I consider why talent management is important, how to make it happen, and who are the main players. This will take us on a journey starting from drawing up a talent strategy and identifying its success criteria, through the different aspects of assessing, developing and deploying people, to finally considering the different roles business leaders, line managers and HR have in making talent important for everyone.

References

1 Michaels, E, Handfield-Jones, H and Axelrod, B (1997) *The War for Talent*, Harvard Business School Press, Boston, Mass
2 CIPD (2006) *Talent Management: Understanding the dimensions*, www.cipd.co.uk/researchinsights
3 Hirsch, W (2009) *Talent management: practical issues in implementation*, Institute of Employment Studies, UK
4 Official Google blog
5 Cohn, J, Katzenbach, J and Vlak, G (2008) Innovation, *Harvard Business Review*
6 Hamel, G (2009) *Building leadership capability for change*, podcast episode 32, www.cipd.co.uk
7 Lawler III, E (2008) *Talent: Making People Your Competitive Advantage*, Jossey Bass, San Francisco

The new world organization

02

My approach to talent management is strategic and inclusive and as much about behaviours and values as about systems and processes. It is strategic because it means looking ahead and aligning individual development with future organizational needs. It is inclusive because it recognizes that decisions and actions that will be pivotal to success may occur anywhere in the organization.

Inclusive talent management is a concept, as well as a set of practices. It is more than aiming to harness people's talents and help them be the best they can be, though that is part of it. It is more than having people available to fill key roles, though that too is part of it. It is a way of thinking and doing things that gets to the heart of relationships with the organization. It includes people in the vision and direction of the business, so that they actively seek to create opportunities and make them happen. It includes people in decisions that are made about them, or that affect them, so that leadership and management are two-way and people have more control over their destinies. It is also about how staff, line managers and HR work together to create an innovative, creative, skilled and adaptable workforce that is willing to learn.

In the previous chapter, I made the case for this approach to talent management as the response to the unprecedented demands of a rapidly changing and ever more challenging business world. In this chapter, I turn to the pressures on people and systems within the organization and show how talent management responds to these.

First, I look at the link between talent management and employee engagement. Many studies show that high levels of engagement among the workforce lead to improved business performance. I will examine this and set out data showing that talent management shares many factors with employee engagement. This provides hard evidence, alongside the conceptual approach, to support the business case for talent management. It will also help us understand the roles of individuals, business leaders, line managers and HR in delivering talent management.

There is evidence of a new leadership model emerging, which devolves leadership in the organization around the principle of 'shared vision, values and understanding'. I will discuss how this reflects attitudes in modern society, and look at why behaviours and values are so important in the 'new world' organization, and how they underpin this leadership model.

What is employee engagement?

Intuitively, we would expect that building on the desire to do a good job, which characterizes most people, would improve their individual performance and that this in turn would improve organizational performance. It is not so much that the concept needs proving; it is more about explaining what is required to achieve it and about proving the correlation with business performance.

To help make sense of the many elements that make up this concept, we need to construct a mental model to guide our thinking. This groups the elements of employee effectiveness into three factors: people's ability, their motivation and the opportunity.[1] Ability refers to personal qualities, skills, and knowledge. Individuals are driven by their own inner motivation but this also needs to be directed by effective external management, since individuals will also be unable to exercise their abilities and motivation if their work team is badly coordinated or they are poorly managed. Circumstances also need to permit people to exercise their abilities and motivation. If there is a breakdown of the opportunity factor – let us say there is a shortage of orders or materials, or a machine breaks down – then even the best machine operators will be prevented from achieving high productivity. However, if the operators have high ability and are well motivated, then they are more likely to help the business recover quickly and make up for lost time. It is also reasonable to apply the same model to the overall business simply by aggregating these three factors at the organizational level.

All three factors in this model need to come into play to achieve the benefit of what is commonly referred to as employee engagement. Figure 2.1 illustrates this idea and, for simplicity, it rolls management effectiveness into 'opportunity'.

It is particularly striking how interconnected all this is. Opportunity and effective line management reinforce motivation and ability, while even the desired outcome – 'effectiveness' – will reinforce motivation: success breeds high morale. Which elements of this diagram represent employee engagement? Well, it is hard to tease them apart. My entire thesis of talent management builds on the idea that all these processes within the management of organizations are interconnected and need to be treated as an integrated whole. One bit without the other does not work.

With this model in the background, let's now establish how employee engagement is generally defined, and then consider the evidence of its importance to business performance. Employee engagement has been described as 'a positive attitude held by the employee towards the organization and its

FIGURE 2.1   Employee engagement

values. An engaged employee is aware of business context and works with colleagues to improve performance within the job for the benefit of the organization.'[2] It gives rise to the 'degree of discretionary effort employees are willing to apply in their work in the organization' and it recognizes that 'every employee ultimately chooses whether to contribute the minimum levels of performance required (or to sabotage), or to go beyond the minimum required by the post and to offer outstanding effort in their role'.[3]

Why is employee engagement important?

Numerous studies make a persuasive case for how engagement leads to success. No single one has proved this beyond doubt, as proving causality would require comparators where all factors are the same, which is impossible to achieve. However, there are sufficient studies that taken together make a compelling case. These are the findings of some of the larger studies.

Towers Perrin–ISR conducts an annual survey; in 2005 it included a study that looked specifically at levels of engagement at 50 large international companies and sought to correlate these with financial performance. It concluded that companies with high employee engagement levels also experienced a higher operating margin (up to 19 per cent higher), net profit margin, revenue growth and earnings per share (up to 28 per cent higher) than companies with low employee engagement.[4] This does not tell us whether it is the more profitable companies that have higher levels of engagement – through a halo effect – or whether it is the higher levels of engagement that lead to improved performance. But it provides indicative support for the latter notion. Towers Perrin's subsequent surveys reveal similar findings.

In 2006 Gallup examined 23,910 business units and compared top quartile and bottom quartile financial performance with engagement scores. They found that those with engagement scores in the bottom quartile averaged 31–51 per cent more employee turnover, 51 per cent more inventory shrinkage and 62 per cent more accidents. Those with engagement scores in the top quartile averaged 12 per cent higher customer advocacy, 18 per cent higher productivity and 12 per cent higher profitability.[5]

In the same year a second Gallup study of 89 organizations found that the earnings per share growth rate of those with engagement scores in the top quartile was 2.6 times that of organizations with below-average scores.[6] Gallup indicates that higher levels of engagement are strongly related to higher levels of innovation. Fifty-nine per cent of engaged employees say that their job brings out their most creative ideas, against only 3 per cent of disengaged employees.

IES/Work Foundation research found that if organizations increased investment in workplace practices that relate to engagement by just 10 per cent, they would increase profits by £1,500 per employee per year.[7]

The characteristics of employee engagement

The case for creating employee engagement is compelling but what do you have to do to achieve it?

In 2003 the study by Purcell *et al*, *Understanding the People and Performance Link: Unlocking the Black Box* (henceforth referred to as the Black Box study) concluded that 'there is strong evidence in a number of organizations that, when effectively managed, some HR policies and practices had positive associations with performance', though the study also acknowledged that 'it is impossible to isolate the impact of HR policies and practices from other factors, such as technology or market fluctuations'.[8] The study's main objective was not to prove the link but to investigate its characteristics. It identified 11 policies and practices that make a difference: recruitment and selection; training and development; career opportunity; communications; involvement in decision making; team working; appraisal; pay; job security; job challenge/job autonomy; work–life balance. These findings are supported by the IES/Work Foundation research.

Is employee engagement something new or simply a repackaging of previous ideas? First, new technology has opened up more sophisticated opportunities to collect and process data. This provides us with the possibility to test assumptions and provide hard data to measure success and identify business improvements. It enables us to go beyond our previous aim of retaining people longer to making people more productive while they are with us, as well as stay longer. So in a sense, employee engagement is a technological measurement process, which provides evidence of what we have to do to drive business success. As the saying goes, 'If you can measure it, then you can manage it.' Second, employee engagement has evolved from previous management theories, which emphasize the importance of employee commitment. The distinction is that earlier management theory tended to be one-way – what to do to gain commitment – whereas employee engagement is a two-way interaction between employer and employee. The following indicators of an engaged workforce illustrate this. I have derived them from the studies discussed above and have proven them as practical tools with clients.

Engaged employees:

- feel respected and treated fairly in areas such as pay, benefits, job security and opportunity;
- know that they are listened to and that their opinions count;
- understand how they contribute to organizational goals and success;
- feel proud of their jobs and their accomplishments;
- know what the future might hold for them and how they might be supported to get there;
- enjoy good, productive relationships with their co-workers.

Managers should regularly ask themselves what they are doing to meet these indicators. It cannot be emphasized enough that their delivery demands meaningful conversations between individuals and their managers about performance and careers, where individuals are able to contribute their input to decisions, and line managers give specific and considered feedback. For HR these are critical indicators for tracking the effectiveness of your talent management practices.

The link between talent management and employee engagement

The attraction to organizations of the effects of engagement is obvious; it potentially enables the organization to increase employee effort and productivity and improve team working, as well as reduce turnover and absenteeism, without increasing salary costs. It maximizes the value of the organization's investment in people.

Talent management has a significant impact on employee engagement. This is shown by the fact that the core indicators of employee engagement listed above are also those of talent management. This becomes even clearer if we list the key ideas of talent management and see how they mirror indicators of employee engagement. Talent management is a process that:

- *Delivers capabilities that the organization needs, when and where it needs them.* The process of achieving this clearly requires a review of the needs of the organization and its goals but it also demands conversations with employees to answer their questions about: How am I doing? How will I be rewarded? What does the future hold? How will I get there? How are we doing as a team? This is not just about identifying capabilities, potential and aspiration but also about broader issues of retaining, motivating and developing staff in order to deliver those capabilities. Satisfying these issues matches several of the indicators of employee engagement. 'Feeling proud of your job and accomplishments' and 'feeling respected and treated fairly in areas such as pay, benefits, job security and opportunity', for example, which are factors in employee engagement, are also factors of motivation that drive retention and are part of the talent management process.

- *Identifies future capabilities that the organization will need and develops people to meet them.* This requires taking a longer-term view of development than is typical, which tends to be one year ahead to fit the performance appraisal cycle. It encourages everyone to think about what is evolving, what is changing and what is driving the business so as to identify capability gaps. It encourages line managers to think about changing skills sets and employee expectations. This helps the individual understand what the future might hold for them and identify a career path. It helps the organization prepare people to meet the challenges of its longer-term business strategy. I will return to these ideas in Chapter 7.

  The process of developing individuals must make them feel better about themselves and about the organization. They appreciate that they are valued and see their worth to the organization being enhanced, which will improve their sense of engagement. Even if personal development improves someone's long-term prospects outside the organization, there is still likely to be this improved sense of engagement in the short term and benefits to the organization as well as the individual. This links to the employee engagement indicator about employees knowing what the future might hold and how they might be supported to get there.

- *Delivers not just individual capabilities but those that are part of what the team does as a unit.* Talent management is as much a mindset as a process. It encourages conversations between line managers and staff, and it encourages sharing of information and ideas, as well as support and collaboration. In this way, it is a main contributor to employee engagement, mapping directly to the factor about enjoying good, productive relationships with co-workers.

- *Creates innovation, resilience and flexibility at all levels of the organization.* The outcomes from the previous attributes should be directed towards achieving innovation, resilience and flexibility. Talent management is not just what you do but how you do it: how you have conversations, how you implement systems. This maps directly to factors that lead to high employee engagement: knowing your opinions count and are listened to, knowing how you contribute to organizational goals and success.

This demonstrates how the factors you address in talent management are also those that contribute to high levels of employee engagement.

How do we bring talent policies to life?

The main lever to bring talent policies to life is the quality of the relationships people have with their top leadership, their line manager and with each other. In Chapter 9 we look closely at these relationships and at how a talent management strategy can support them. For now, I would like to consider the evidence to support this contention.

There is much commonality among the surveys about which factors lead to higher engagement levels, and much of it points to the role of the line manager. The Black Box study found that front-line managers exercise a strong influence over the level of discretionary effort that an individual directs to their job.[9] Some managers encourage people to be responsible for their own jobs whereas others stifle initiative through controlling or autocratic behaviour. Similar findings emerge from the Institute of Employment Studies (IES) research, which concludes, 'The line manager clearly has a very important role in fostering employees' sense of involvement and value – an observation that is completely consistent with IES's research in many different areas of HR practice and employment, all of which point to the critical importance of the employee–manager relationship.'[10] That 'People join companies but they leave managers' is an often-quoted assertion that reinforces this point.

These surveys also achieve consensus over what line managers need to do to create an engaged employee. This can be summed up as: help and support employees to take more responsibility for how they do their jobs, provide developmental opportunities, enable people to see how they contribute to organizational goals, seek out and listen to people's views, listen, lead and learn. In other words: talent management.

It would be disingenuous to ascribe the achievement of employee engagement solely to the behaviour or competence of individual line managers, as they too are affected by the system in which they operate and the way they themselves are managed. Towers Perrin's research found that while many people are keen to contribute more at work, the culture of their organizations, as well as the behaviour of their managers, discourages them from doing so.[11] Similar conclusions emerge from the Black Box research:

'Organizations that have a strong, shared culture with guiding principles for behaviour embedded into practice over time' were revealed by the research to have been more successful.[12] These findings strongly support one of my central themes that I develop in the next chapter: the importance of aligning vision, values, strategy and behaviour.

To recap so far, we have seen compelling evidence that business performance increases when people are engaged with the organization, and we have established that talent management is the main driver of employee engagement. We have also discussed the outcomes talent management must achieve for the organization and have seen that how these outcomes are achieved not only requires 'bundles of HR practices', but effective delivery of these by line managers.

However, if it is what line managers do, combined with strategies, systems and processes, that delivers talent management, it is organizational culture and values that are the glue to make it stick. This brings us to our next topic: a discussion of leadership and organizational culture.

Leadership models that enhance employee engagement

It is not surprising that recognizing the importance of leadership characteristics has led writers to think about failure and to ponder 'destructive' or 'toxic' leadership, which describes undesirable leadership behaviours. Toxic leadership is a term originally coined by Marcia Whicker[13] and taken further by Lipman-Blumen.[14] It refers to individuals who exhibit a range of behaviours characterized by selfishness that demoralize those they manage, leads to disengagement and sacrifices employees or whole organizations for ego and self-aggrandizement. Corporate scandals such as Enron and the near collapse of RBS illustrate weaknesses in the 'heroic' or 'great man' leadership models. Research carried out by Tosi *et al*, which finds no link between organizational success and the perceived charisma of the CEO, supports this critical view.[15] In place of the 'heroic' models, alternatives that include 'being open and considerate of others' and demonstrating 'humility' are being cited as desirable. We also see leadership models that emphasize the distribution of leadership throughout the organization, as well as the importance of shared vision, values and understanding.

This new approach to leadership highlights the convergence of two important trends in the 'new world' discussed in the last chapter. First, it seems that people in the new world are less willing to accept the 'command and control' model of management from on high by the 'heroic leader'. It seems to be becoming less common and not to be working very well. The second fact is that, as discussed in the first chapter, the pace and complexity of change in our societies and business environment seem to be encouraging innovation and flexibility at all levels of the organization. In turn, this makes a more devolved leadership style desirable so that companies can cope effectively in these circumstances.

The writer who has perhaps done most to promote this view of leadership is Jim Collins, whose work, *Good to Great*,[16] has been hailed as a classic. He investigated over 1,400 organizations quoted on the US Stock Exchange, controlling for economic factors and size among other variables. He focused on those who moved their organizations from solidly 'good' performance to 'great' performance and who maintained this position for at least 15 years. He identified two common characteristics: one, the steadfast belief of the chief executive that their company would be the best in the field; and the second, their 'deep personal humility'. The first of these critical factors reflects a strategic approach to business. The latter characteristic reflects a way of managing: it emphasizes the role of the team and identifies the leadership job as enabling that team to perform effectively.

Let us be clear what we mean by leadership here. At the top level of the organization it deals with overall strategy and vision and values, as discussed before. It is a subset of the management process, which is a concept little changed since F W Taylor, the earliest management commentator, developed his theories of scientific management. Taylor described management as being about planning, organizing people and resources and about control. His emphasis was on efficiency and administration and, in an era when this was achieved through a 'command and control' approach, this was how the line manager managed. However, his work did not focus on the 'how' of getting people to do things efficiently, much less on the 'how' of creating an innovative organization. As society has changed, so this 'how' has become a much more important consideration in management, which brings us to leadership.

Our ideas of business leadership grew from the work of behavioural scientists in the 1960s. They introduced the idea that influencing people by virtue of personal attributes and behaviours was important to management success. At first this notion worked within 'command and control' structures, with line managers influencing to gain commitment and enthusiasm. Real, full-blown leadership – 'driving change', 'setting direction', 'interacting with stakeholders' – was the preserve of people at the top. Since the 1960s the issues discussed in the last chapter – rapid change and competitiveness in the business environment, the emergence of the knowledge worker and of the information age and, now, of the innovation age – fomented change and have put behaviours centre stage. These are behaviours related to learning, adaptability, flexibility and team working. They are also the different leadership behaviours required at different levels of the organization and for different roles. For example, a professional expert, though not a line manager, may be required to lead and direct a significant piece of change, while interacting with and managing others across organizational boundaries – which illustrates that anyone, anywhere, may be required to move in and out of leadership roles at different times.

The devolved leadership model also recognizes that innovation and creativity can come from anywhere in the organization. It allows for individuals anywhere within it to have knowledge and understanding that is a valuable input into decision making. MacBeath argues that 'distributed leadership is premised on trust, implies a mutual acceptance of one another's leadership potential, requires formal leaders to "let go" some of their control and authority, and favours consultation and consensus over command and control'.[17] It is not a zero-sum game, where developing others diminishes the power of those at the top, but 'one where each can mutually reinforce the other'.

What is the most effective way of leading people?

The importance of 'behaviours' as the means to bring about a culture change was addressed initially through the concept of the learning organization. This is a theory of organizations as 'learning systems' in which success depends on two key skills – learning continuously and giving direction. I believe this idea succeeded, but only to a limited degree; it helped change attitudes and get individuals to recognize the importance of learning. It helped them see learning as something to take control of, as opposed to it being something that is 'done' to them through being sent on a training course. However, this has had little impact on the way people and relationships are managed in the organization. This role has been taken by coaching, which has increasingly gained hold as being the most effective way of managing people and building working relationships.

A CIPD survey in July 2009 found that 90 per cent of the 598 respondents reported that coaching was taking place in their organizations, delivered primarily by line managers supported by internal or external coaches. The report concludes that 'coaching is increasingly being delivered by line management'.[18] This correlates with ACE's International HR Barometer, whose 598 international respondents cited 'developing line managers' coaching skills' a priority for 2010.[19]

CIPD research also shows that a coaching style of management delivers benefits that are manifested in better team relationships, enhanced self-confidence and more general improvements to engagement, flexibility and commitment.[20] A coaching style of management is not about 'being the boss', giving directions, telling people how they should have done it or jumping in with the answer. Rather, a manager's role today is to enable, encourage and facilitate so that staff have a sense of control over their own work and their own time, so they identify their own options and solutions to problems, so they are involved in decisions and so they learn and develop. A manager may also work with an employee on a more formal coaching basis, perhaps to help that person develop their knowledge or acquire a new skill or responsibility.

It is unsurprising that developing line managers' ability to coach is gaining such importance, as 'command and control' styles have a practical drawback: with leaner organizations, managers do not have time to micromanage and, with wider spans of control the norm, they may have insufficient detailed understanding of the technical aspects of various jobs. Moreover, coaching styles are transferable to different situations and, increasingly, line managers must achieve results through people over whom they have no direct authority. In these situations they must influence by using coaching skills rather than command.

The devolved leadership model, whose characteristics are 'shared vision, values and understanding', is the next step. Using coaching styles as the main delivery mechanism, this leadership model enables decisions and actions important to success to occur anywhere in the organization. It recognizes that innovation requires teamwork and collaboration and that people at all levels must be able to create and spot opportunities. It also takes account of structural pressures that are blurring organizational boundaries and reporting lines.

These are the trends that talent management is responding to, and they are also the trends that talent management must set.

The way we do things around here

For talent management and devolved leadership to flourish, they must be supported by the organizational culture.

We all know what we mean by culture but most of us have difficulty defining it precisely. It is broadly the shared values and the collection of different behaviours that, taken together, comprise 'the way we do things around here'. These can include rituals and customs such as going for a drink with colleagues on a Friday night as well as interacting through formal management meetings. It can include the way one is expected to behave on these occasions. It can be built on shared memories and experiences but that does not preclude new colleagues being inducted into the behaviours without having shared those experiences.

Organizational culture can be complex and can vary across the organization. As Schein, an acknowledged expert in corporate culture points out, 'Wherever a group has enough common experience, a culture begins to form.'[21] Culture can reside at all levels in any system: a country has its own culture, as does a whole industry. There may be an organizational culture but, undoubtedly, there will also be a distinct culture for each department, group or team. Culture can also change over time. As it affects the way people do things and make decisions, sometimes changes need to be helped along to ensure the organization has the right culture in the right place.

According to Schein, 'There is now abundant evidence that corporate culture makes a difference to corporate performance.' This is a compelling argument for analysing culture and, where appropriate, seeking to manage its development in a particular direction. To return to an earlier point, here again these are trends that talent management is responding to, and they are also trends that talent management must set.

Researchers agree that culture is more than 'shared values', yet values are often considered integral to culture. Hofstede used the metaphor of an onion to describe the manifestation of culture at different levels. On the outside layer lie symbols (ie words, gestures, and objects), heroes (ie iconic representation of the admired in the culture), rituals (ie collective activities and teachings), and finally values as the core of the culture.[22] Certainly, values have come to be a shorthand way of describing the culture. I use the term in this way throughout this book.

Organizational values

Organizational values define the standards that guide the behaviour of individuals within the organization. As Rokeach claimed, values are the rules that help us make decisions in life.[23] Without them, individuals will pursue behaviours in line with their own value systems, which may lead to behaviours that the organization does not wish to encourage. Values reflect both current reality and aspiration for a company and make a distinctive statement not just about how the company works but about what it thinks really matters. This distinctive statement reflects the personality of the organization. It is a unique way of pulling the organization together and also creates differentiation, a critical factor in competitive markets.

Creating shared values, however, presents the philosophical problem that values are something an individual holds but might not be shared by a group of people. 'Values are considered by researchers to be the beliefs that are held individually or collectively, perceived consciously or unconsciously, communicated explicitly (verbally articulated) or implicitly (symbolically), used as the criteria for cognitive, affective, or behavioural judgments to guide our choices out of available options, as they influence society, while society influences them.'[24] They correlate with our motivations, attitudes and behaviours. They are crucial qualities that represent culture and which are shaped by the many influences on us, especially early in our lives, and of course one of the principal influences is national culture.

We tend to encounter a series of micro-cultures in organizations where different norms and values prevail, depending upon a range of factors including the type of work undertaken and the geographic and physical location. As Handy and Harrison and also Stokes suggest, what is important is to have the right culture in the right place: one that suits the work and the way it is done.[25] They describe micro-cultures across the organization, but they also describe an overarching organizational culture. This notion of the layering of cultures with one prevailing and overarching culture is important to a pragmatic consideration of how to define values and make them mean something across the organization. This is important to talent management, which should be implemented so that it is relevant to and conscious of the values of the organization.

Giving values meaning

It is useful to take stock of what you want to achieve by having corporate values. It is likely that as an HR or organizational leader you seek a work environment that encourages behaviour that has positive effects on stakeholders and the community. You are probably aware that an increasing number of customers, employees, regulators and legislators are paying attention to the impact of organizations on society. They will support an organization whose values they identify with: whether because they support its ethical standards or because the brand image suits them sufficiently to buy the products or join as an employee. Values, therefore, reflect what your organization stands for: they encapsulate its personality and link it with its various stakeholders.

Douglas Macgregor states that organizations that have succeeded in engaging everyone around clearly discernible values do not simply proclaim their values; they immerse their managers as well as their employees in the ideology to an obsessive degree.[26] New members learn the values of the organization through their initial socialization processes. Many organizations, such as the *Guardian* newspaper and the BBC have long-held values, and employees are well versed and immersed in them. They act as constant reference points against which people determine policy, interpret challenges and dilemmas and take decisions.

The following case study illustrates how the Guardian Media Group (GMG) uses its values as a reference point for all employees on a wide range of issues. They act as a focus to pull people together and help to establish a corporate identity and company loyalty; they help people know how to behave; they set boundaries within which people can work – that way you don't need a 'do' and 'don't do' list, or someone to say you can or cannot do something: it is obvious and falls into place.

GMG has a broad portfolio of businesses and investments. Its core business is Guardian News and Media (GNM), which publishes the *Guardian* and the *Observer* as well as the guardian.co.uk website. GMG is owned by the Scott Trust Ltd.

The idea that businesses have obligations to the society in which they operate is often thought of as a relatively new phenomenon even though many businesses, particularly those founded by Quakers in 19th-century Britain, espoused this view. At GMG an awareness of the wider responsibilities of business has always been at the heart of what they do. The *Manchester Guardian* was created to support social reform in the early 19th century, and the ethos of public service has been part of its DNA ever since. The editor C P Scott summed this up in his 1921 leader marking the centenary of the paper, in which he asserted that newspapers have 'a moral as well as material existence'. He listed the essential attributes he believed should form the character of a newspaper. He wrote that the most precious possession was 'honesty, cleanness (integrity), courage, fairness, and a sense of duty to the reader and the community'. The Scott Trust later adopted these values as its own; they continue to inform the way in which GMG runs its business, operating GNM as a commercial enterprise while always seeking to adhere to principles of decency and public service.[27]

Since then, these values have acted as a guiding light and clear reference point in shaping the style and nature of the newspaper and of the group as a place to work. Alison Hall, head of change management at GNM, says: 'People choose to work here because of the values. You know what is right and what is wrong and what fits with the paper's ethos. It does not need policing.' This clarity enables people to adapt and act quickly, whether in formulating policy or pursuing a story.

This values-driven approach is illustrated by the response of GNM editor-in-chief Alan Rusbridger to a question during a visit to Norway in June 2009 when he revealed that he does not read all the tweets from journalists before they are published: 'I was told that this could not happen in Norway as the editor-in-chief would insist on reading all content,' says Rusbridger. 'We are probably ahead of others as we devolve a great deal of responsibility and freedom to our reporters. The idea of journalists publishing directly is not a shocking one for us.'[28]

This last example shows how clear values facilitate trust on the part of the managers and, as a result, leadership is devolved to where and when it matters.

Where organizations do not have the long-held traditions of GNM, identifying values and making them mean the same things to everyone can be problematic. One such problem being that organizations usually, and perhaps inevitably, choose their values from a small set of words or phrases that can equally mean a lot or nothing. At worst, empty phrases give rise to cynicism and discontent, as people find the organization does not live up to its promises. The most common 'value words' used in organizations are: openness, fairness, integrity, honesty, respect, customer focus, team orientation and creativity. Given these difficulties:

- How do you identify values and ensure everyone shares their meaning? How can you achieve this while also retaining flexibility for differences across departments, business units and geographical location, where needs may be rather different?

- How do you ensure that these words are not empty platitudes and really mean something?

We can draw some answers to these questions from Standard Chartered Bank and GMG.

Standard Chartered's values take the form of five descriptors: courageous, responsive, international, creative, trustworthy. The bank invested considerable time and effort into identifying these values through discussion and workshops and using consultancy support to facilitate discussions. Then, having homed in on just five words that might be expected to be subject to infinite interpretation and confusion, they established a process to make sure that everyone understands and 'lives' them.

Their unusual approach emerged from the organization's cultural propensity to conversation. As with all their talent processes, Standard Chartered places considerable emphasis on the importance of conversations. Line managers discuss values with their direct reports and within teams. Everyone has the opportunity to identify what one of these values, or descriptors, means to them and what it means for the team. This enables Standard Chartered to establish a 'one bank' identity across the world, while allowing for behaviours associated with a value to be different for each part of the business; it also allows for cultural interpretations of the values across the world. So, for example, 'courageous' might be taken to encourage a little more risk taking in one division or a more individualistic approach in another. Similarly, the descriptor 'international' might just be a statement of organizational fact in one context, but in another it may encourage different functions and business areas to seek out best-practice techniques across the various offices of the bank.

At Standard Chartered, people's performance appraisal review includes how they have upheld their values, as well as whether they have achieved their performance objectives; and evidence is required to substantiate their claims. There are two parts to a performance appraisal rating: achievement of objectives, and upholding values. A low rating for values will pull down someone's bonus award, even if the person has exceeded their objectives.

At GMG, Carolyn Gray, group HR director, receives reports from the HR directors of the individual businesses on various aspects of HR. This includes evidence of how these HR activities are aligned with Scott Trust values. She then presents an overall report to the GMG board, including how effectively values have been upheld. What is striking here is how it remains important to continually refer to values and be conscious of them, even when they have been in place since 1921.

To answer our earlier questions, these case studies help us conclude:

- To make values stick, you must consciously work at embedding them.

- The key to establishing 'shared values' is to constantly articulate and evaluate behaviour. It is not easy for people to change their values, especially when these are associated with their national culture, but they can change their behaviour – and it is how people behave that brings the values to life. Discussing these behaviours with reference to values will help you put a shared meaning on values, while also allowing for cultural adaptations.

- Check that your values are promoted through the actions and words of the people at the top. Facilitate this where necessary.
- Check that your values are upheld consistently through all policies and practices.

'Shared values' represent an organization's long-term view of the world; that is, you cannot change them too frequently – you need to make sure you define them properly but then hold your nerve with them and really embed them to reap long-term benefits.

I advocate developing a talent management strategy. Drawing up a strategy will engage you in conversations around the business, which lead to insights that do not often emerge when you are caught up in the day to day. These conversations are opportunities for reinforcing your values and generating a shared meaning. One aim of a talent strategy is to join up your people processes and integrate these with business strategy so that your processes transmit consistent messages and influence consistent behaviour. This too is instrumental in creating 'shared values'. As we saw earlier, a role of talent management is to drive the culture and the behaviours that will lead to sustainable success for your business. In an ideal world, you will have the active support for this from your senior management team, or indeed your values will already be in place. Where this is not the case, be especially conscious of the behaviours your policies may drive. For example, if you need to drive teamwork, or encourage accountability, communicate how a particular initiative will help achieve this. Eventually, as behaviours develop, cultural values will become more evident and will take on a shared meaning.

As Charlie Mayfield, chairman of the John Lewis Partnership, wrote in *The Times*, 'putting emphasis on values is also a recipe for commercial success. Companies that focus most on maximizing profit are often not the most profitable. That's especially true over time.'[29]

LEARNING POINTS

- Talent management has a significant impact on employee engagement. The factors that employees share can be measured and tracked. They make the case for talent management.

- Behaviours can be encapsulated in a statement of values – but values don't just happen; they must be articulated and managed constantly. Consistent behaviour leads to 'shared values', which help develop an organization's identity.

- Line manager behaviour brings talent policies to life. It is especially important that line managers hold 'meaningful conversations' with people. These are conversations about performance and careers that give open and honest feedback and recognition for good work.

- 'Command and control' structures and styles of management run counter to employee expectations and are becoming impractical to maintain. A powerful alternative is a coaching style of management where people are supported and challenged, rather than told what to do. They are led through shared vision, values and understanding.

References

1 Purcell, J *et al* (2003) *Understanding the People and Performance Link: Unlocking the Black Box*, CIPD, London

2 Robinson, D, Perryman, S and Hayday, S (2004) The drivers of employee engagement, *Institute for Employment Studies*, Report 408, April

3 Alimo-Metcalfe, B and Alban-Metcalfe, J (2009) *Engaging Leadership*, CIPD Insight Report

4 Towers Perrin (2005) *Reconnecting with employees: quantifying the value of engaging your workforce*, Towers Perrin, London

5 Harter, J K *et al* (2006) Gallup Q12 Meta-Analysis

6 Gallup Organization (2006) Engagement predicts earnings per share

7 Tamkin, P, Cowling, M and Hunt, W (2008) People and the bottom line, *Institute for Employment Studies*, Report 448

8 Purcell, J *et al* (2003) *Understanding the People and Performance Link: Unlocking the Black Box*, CIPD, London

9 *ibid*

10 Tamkin, P, Cowling, M and Hunt, W (2008) People and the bottom line, *Institute for Employment Studies*, Report 448

11 Towers Perrin (2005) *Global workforce study*, Towers Perrin, London

12 *ibid*

13 Whicker, M L (1996) *Toxic leaders: When organizations go bad*, Quorum Books, Westport, CT
14 Lipman-Blumen, J (2004) *The Allure of Toxic Leaders: Why We Follow Destructive Bosses and Corrupt Politicians – and How We Can Survive Them*, Oxford University Press, USA
15 Tosi, H L, Misangyi, V F and Fanelli, A (2004) CEO charisma, compensation, and firm performance, *Leadership Quarterly*, **15** (3), June, pp 405–20
16 Collins, J (2001) *Good to Great: Why Some Companies Make the Leap ... and Others Don't*, Random House
17 MacBeath, J (2005) Leadership as distributed: a matter of practice, *School Leadership and Management*, **25** (4), pp 349–66
18 CIPD (2009) *Taking the Temperature of Coaching*, Coaching survey, CIPD, London
19 *ACE International HR Barometer* (2009) www.network-ace.com
20 CIPD (2009) *Taking the Temperature of Coaching*, Coaching survey, CIPD, London
21 Schein, E H (1999) *The Corporate Culture Survival Guide*, Jossey-Bass, San Francisco
22 Hofstede, G (2001) *Culture's Consequences: comparing values, behaviors, institutions, and organizations across nations*, 2nd edn, Sage Publications
23 Rokeach, M (1968) *Beliefs, Attitudes and Values*, Jossey-Bass, San Francisco; and by the same author, A theory of organization and change within value–attitude systems, *Journal of Social Issues*, **24** (January 1968), pp 13–33
24 http://www.allacademic.com/meta/p_mla_apa_research_citation/2/3/4/5/9/pages234591/p234591-4.php
25 Handy, C (1995) *Gods of Management: The Changing Work of Organizations*, Arrow, London; Harrison, R and Stokes, H (1992) *Diagnosing Organizational Culture*, Pfeiffer, San Francisco
26 Macgregor, D A (1997) *Breaking the Phalanx*, Praeger, Westport; http://www.usafa.edu/isme/JSCOPE99/Bell99.html Impact of Policies on Organizational Values and Culture LTC William F Bell, USA
27 www.gmgplc.co.uk
28 *Living Our Values*, sustainability report 2008–9, the *Guardian* and the *Observer*
29 Mayfield, C (2010) The private sector can learn from co-ops too, *The Times*, 3 March

Setting the strategic direction

03

In the previous chapter, we discussed how the leadership model is transforming from one where leadership comes from the top to a devolved model that promotes shared vision, values and understanding throughout the workforce. This does not detract from the top leadership responsibilities for setting the strategic direction and maintaining overall control. Rather, it empowers people lower down the organization to spot opportunities, contribute their ideas and take extra responsibility for devolved decision making. The talent management flowchart in Appendix B shows the flow between vision and values and the talent strategy and its component parts.

The process of developing and then communicating organizational strategy helps to create a shared understanding of the goals and direction of the business. Talent management also has a role in this through linking each person's performance and development with those business goals.

I start this chapter with a general look at strategy, so that we can work from a common understanding of it. I then turn specifically to talent management and how to set the overall direction of a talent strategy, and discuss the benefits of doing so.

Defining strategy

The Red Queen's race in Lewis Carroll's *Through the Looking-Glass* involves the Red Queen and Alice constantly running but remaining in the same spot:

'Well, in our country,' said Alice, still panting a little, 'you'd generally get to somewhere else – if you run very fast for a long time, as we've been doing.'
'A slow sort of country!' said the Queen. 'Now, here, you see, it takes all the running you can do, to keep in the same place. If you want to get somewhere else, you must run at least twice as fast as that.'

This story illustrates the perils of having no strategy – you run fast but don't get anywhere. What you need is objectives – knowing where you are running to – and a plan to get there, which is your strategy. Of course your strategy needs to take account of your capabilities – how fast you can run – and the obstacles you might meet – competitors, legislation, change generally. Your strategy will include some contingency planning, in case one of the roads along the way gets blocked, the terrain changes or an alternative path is better.

However, this raises a number of questions. How do you formulate this strategy? How do you choose goals? What are the important characteristics of a strategy that you need to know if you are to choose a good path?

Why does a strategy matter?

You could argue that strategy doesn't matter. Michael Porter, one of the foremost thinkers on the subject, argues that even very successful Japanese companies often exist without strategies. He suggests that many have competed and grown by increasing operational effectiveness – they just get better and better at what they do. However, eventually they reach what he describes as the productivity frontier, where they are doing everything as well as they can.[1]

With the fierce competition that characterizes Japanese markets the rival firms will soon spot a process improvement and copy it. If it is protected by a patent or copyright, then one firm will have an advantage for a while but all the other firms will be trying to find another way of achieving the same improvement that is not protected. As Porter says, this process of continuous improvement unwittingly draws all firms to imitation and homogeneity.

If nobody can significantly improve the quality of their product, the efficiency of production, the speed of new product introduction or the low cost of distribution, then how do they compete with their rivals who have also reached this frontier? Doesn't it mean that they can only compete on price and then, since everyone else is doing the same, that any benefits are captured by customers and not by the firm itself? He puts forward examples of market-leading Japanese companies that have produced unsatisfactory returns over many years. The people who have benefited from all their fierce competition with each other are their customers and distributors, not their shareholders.

So strategy, if it is different from operational effectiveness, does seem to matter, and matter a lot, but that brings us back to 'What is it?'

Characteristics of strategy

After centuries of debate most theologians settled on trying to describe God through His attributes or even by what He is not. Similarly with strategy it is probably easier to describe it by its characteristics.

Businesses can be described as a set of activities – the things that the organization does. It buys in particular ways, it processes inputs, it sells, it manages its staff. All of these are activities. You can split these into more detailed activities: within the umbrella of 'selling' you can also include that the business advertises, it runs a sales force, it has a website. You can split these activities further: within running a sales force you can also include activities such as recruiting salespeople, allocating markets to them, managing and rewarding and motivating them, supporting them with systems and procedures, computers, samples, training, etc.

We have said that pursuit of operational effectiveness is not a strategy but is something that you do as a matter of course. Therefore strategy must involve you doing different activities from your competitors, or doing the same activities differently from them, or different activities from those you have done before. It must have a clear purpose and lead you somewhere.

How do you produce a strategy?

Tom Peters famously offered $100 to the first manager who could demonstrate a successful strategy that resulted from a planning process. He has never paid out. However, there are many potential benefits from going through planning processes, including working out what operational things you are going to do as a business, what problems you envisage, how you are going to coordinate activities and where, in the short term, you expect this to take you. Not least, planning processes help communication between people at all levels of the company, facilitating communication of the company vision and objectives.

The downside of the planning process is that it can turn into a dry extension of budgeting, just projected for another two years, which can generate serious cynicism in the staff you are trying to enthuse and motivate. What differentiates planning from budgeting is ideas. If you want a three-year forecast, then it is very likely that the finance department can extend the budget, have a chat with each department to find out what might be new and produce a forecast, with far less effort, that is just as good as getting each department to produce a plan that has to be consolidated centrally. However, the finance department will not be able to come up with the business ideas.

What then turns those plans into strategies is when they are more than just ideas, but are insights. Campbell and Alexander believe that strategy is about 'insights into how to create value' and that 'these insights normally focus on practical issues and point to new ways of doing things ... most of the insights important for strategy formulation reside in the heads of the operating managers ... So how should companies set about developing ... insights[?] ... [A]lmost by definition there is no best way.'[2] However, some sort of planning process would seem like a good way to get these people who are most likely to have the insights to talk about the business issues, to raise their view from all those day-to-day problems and to think about the 'big picture'.

One person's strategy is another person's goal

Let us temporarily put aside the point that a strategy is about insights and use the more conventional, albeit incomplete, usage that strategy is just the means used to attain set goals. It is hard to separate a business's purpose, goals, strategy, tactics – a strategy in one part of the business becomes a goal for another, calling in turn for its own strategy to achieve it. For example, achieving a highly motivated and skilled workforce may be a strategy for an overall business that will help it to achieve a goal that is, say, a dominant market position; but that business strategy is a goal for the HR department and in turn will demand a strategy to achieve it. This does not just occur between different business functions but also as you go down layers in a hierarchy. For example, the board decides that its objective is to achieve a 20 per cent return on investment as a result of winning number one position in a market through positioning the company as the price leader, gaining economies of scale and, by doing so, being able to reduce costs and speed up the product development cycle. Even at this level it is not clear which is object-ive and which strategy. Isn't the objective to be number one? Yes, except that is what gives the economies of scale that allow cost reductions that enable the business to sustain its leadership...

At the level of the production department heads their objective is defi-nitely not to be number one but to reduce costs on the basis of a higher sales forecast. In turn they will think through the means to make this happen, which will be their strategy. The elements of that they in turn will hand down to their team as a series of goals. Similarly there is no clear cut-off between what is a tactic and what is a strategy. Usually we think of something short range and short term as being a tactic while the 'bigger picture' represents strategy. So, in the example given above, if the marketing department organizes a price promotion, that would seem to be short term and therefore a tactic – but if it proves to be one of a series of price promo-tions, then perhaps it is a strategy...

My view is that none of these distinctions matters. Let us redefine strategy slightly. Strategy is a connected series of activities that leads in a coherent direction. That is perfectly compatible with it being driven by insights. It is perfectly compatible with the slightly limited use to indicate a pathway towards an objective and also with Porter's ideas about a sustainable strategy requiring differentiation. It also moves us towards another 'take' on strategy that it is about a vision for the enterprise – taking it in a coherent direction. In order to analyse the situation and come up with ideas and insights we can still use the language of objectives, strategies and tactics but we don't need to worry too much about which category an activity falls into if it is not clear. We can just say we are going to do something in such a way because it conforms to our vision for the enterprise.

This highlights the importance of a strategic approach to talent management so that our activities connect and lead in a coherent direction. It fits with our view of talent management as being about focusing on the long term. It fits also with our view that talent management must generate insights so that people come away from the day to day and develop ideas and understanding that add value.

Which comes first – strategy, objective or vision?

If we accept that it doesn't matter whether an action is a tactic, strategy or objective, then why should it matter which order they come in? It only matters to the extent that it helps us to think the issues through when we are trying to come up with a strategy.

Some businesses will set a clear goal such as market leadership, and everything else they do is a coherent attempt to reach it. But some start with the vision, or the core competence. Core competence originates from Prahalad and Hamel. They highlight this as a source of uniqueness: what the company can do uniquely well, offering a competitive advantage that competitors can't quickly copy.[3] Prahalad and Hamel emphasize three conditions to test if a competence is a true core competence: relevant; difficult to imitate; leveraged to many products and markets. Sometimes the terms 'core capability' or 'the big idea' are used to express the same concept. To me, this concept is about aspiration. In this respect, it is both a goal and a guiding philosophy. I believe the term 'vision' encapsulates this meaning well, and it is this term I use throughout this book.

Apple is a prime example of an organization whose vision seems to have shaped its innovation strategy since its inception. To a long-standing and enthusiastic user of Apple products, this vision seems to revolve around the goal of shaping the technology to the customer's needs, instead of forcing the user to adapt to the technology. It also expresses a design philosophy that starts with the belief that the purpose of the design is to create things that benefit people. Keeping true to this vision has seen Apple evolve from a small computer company to a phenomenally successful mobile devices and computer company, whose products define a generation and a lifestyle.

Understanding and developing your vision is all about focus, recognizing where your customers value your uniqueness, where your competitors cannot catch up, and learning to stop being all things to everyone.

Michael Porter discusses a successful US low-cost airline and argues that all its activities are aligned with the concept of being a low-cost airline. Choosing to use the same planes throughout its fleet is directed to reduce maintenance costs, speed up turnaround times at departure gates, ensure its planes and crews can be easily substituted with each other – all of which reduce operating costs. Similarly, decisions not to supply free meals, to limit how tickets can be bought, etc, are also the result of pursuing the strategic direction.[4] No doubt this and other low-cost airlines in Europe also have objectives such as return on sales but these come after the decision to be a low-cost airline.

Too often HR activities are not connected in this way. They give out conflicting messages, do not have a clear purpose, they are bolted on rather than integrated into HR and business strategy. Take this actual, but also typical, case of an organization that launched a 360-degree feedback programme.[5] The way this was set out was little more than throwing another idea into the organization. It didn't show a clear link to the business context or to organizational values, neither did it link to other people processes. Moreover, no thought had been given to what role line managers would have or how the exercise would fit with how the organization wanted people to be managed. It wasn't part of a coherent strategy. Not surprisingly, it was perceived in the organization as HR ticking boxes again. While I think there is always a case for increasing what the organization offers people by way of development and support, I also think that this piecemeal approach fails on several counts.

First and foremost, it fails to link with the business strategy. On the one hand, you could argue that people will make this leap themselves and think, 'This will help me provide a better service to my customers.' However, if it had been thought through and set against a business case, it might have become clear that there were other programmes already in existence in the organization that better served this purpose. Developing those further would have cost less, and possibly brought higher gains. Second, this was a new initiative that had only a tenuous link to other people programmes. This not only wasted previous investment but also lost the goodwill and expertise of those in the organization who had given time and energy to the earlier programme, only to find that there was now a new flavour of the month. Third, it missed an opportunity to articulate clearly what the organization stood for as an employer, how it would make itself a great place to work, how it would reinforce its values and drive forward as a business. Fourth, no thought had been given to the involvement of line managers in the process and how it would help them manage their staff. As a result, it was more likely to add to their load rather than lighten or support it. Last, it did not carry a strategic message from either the HR director or the CEO. This meant it was perceived as 'just another initiative', with people thinking, 'Why should I bother, if it is not going to be noticed and my effort will not be recognized?'

Common problems caused by an uncoordinated approach

An ad hoc, uncoordinated approach to talent management leads to many problems in the organization. As a result, the organization suffers from the following:

- Confusing employer brand promise.
- Promises made at recruitment are not always kept.
- Difficulty in establishing priorities.
- People's energies and talents are misdirected.
- Poor teamwork and high conflict across different teams in the organization.
- Insufficient internal moves and promotions.
- People see reward and recognition as being about increased pay and promotion only.
- People confuse tasks, responsibilities and accountabilities.
- Higher than desirable staff turnover.

This impacts on the business through a confusing brand promise to customers, lower levels of customer satisfaction and lower levels of employee engagement:

- Loose connections.
- Often unclear what the organization is rewarding.
- Setting of goals and objectives varies across the organization.
- Learning, development and their objectives are rarely included in the strategic plan.
- Quality of performance management conversations varies across the organization.
- Opinions differ within the management team regarding defining and assessing levels of performance.
- Consequently, the organization does not know who are its high or poor performers.
- The organization is unable to track people to know who is able to perform what role, either now or in the future.
- High performers feel unrecognized and poor performers continue to underperform.
- Senior management conversations focus on sales, production, finance or service, rarely on people.

- Behaviour in the organization is often out of sync with supposed values.
- People are recruited on the basis of their skills and experience, not on their behaviours.
- Good people management is not rewarded.
- Systems are bureaucratic and restrain rather than guide.
- The organization becomes process driven and people hide behind process rather than using judgement.

Making connections

If we accept the view that strategy adds value by creating insights and that it is a connected series of activities, it is not hard to see that the approach taken with the 360-degree exercise is not strategic and it fails to add value. It certainly does not help you develop organizational values in line with a clear vision. Imagine an organization pulled in all directions by half a dozen uncoordinated HR initiatives and programmes, as in Figure 3.1; then imagine the same organization pushed in one direction by several coordinated programmes – it just seems obvious to me which is more effective.

FIGURE 3.1   Making connections

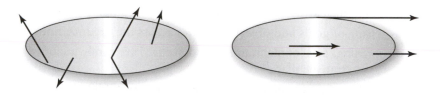

A few years ago, I worked with a leading professional services firm on establishing what they termed a 'high-performance culture'. A performance improvement review of the firm showed they were not particularly effective at managing people. They hadn't previously needed to be. They had become successful through their technical and specialist skills and knowledge. They attracted clients and also new recruits for this reason. Since their competitors were all similarly technically focused, there was no pressure to change. However, the cracks were starting to show. Previously, the firm had grown continuously and there were always enough opportunities to satisfy their ambitious population. Not only was that situation starting to change, but people's expectations were changing too. People were now questioning how long it would take them to reach partner level and were querying whether it was a goal worth achieving. People were also becoming more demanding, they expected to be continually developed and challenged, and to be well managed. It was no longer enough to pay people well and expect them to work all hours with the lure of a partnership at the end. The challenge was to identify the people the firm wanted to retain for future partnership, but also to make a shorter-term career with the firm be seen as a valuable route to securing outstanding opportunities outside. More effective people management was clearly the way to achieving this. Practices and policies, however, gave out contrasting messages. For example, performance appraisal and promotion were based on utilization rates and client success. In explaining criteria for promotion to partner, people were advised to reduce their internally focused activity and increase their client focus if they 'wanted to get on here'. Little or no emphasis was placed on people management skills when recruiting, there were no role models in the organization for excellence in people skills. Most managers took the view that spending more time on people management reduced time with clients. In a culture change programme, driven by HR but owned and actively promoted by the managing partner, the firm set about redefining the role of people management leaders to be regarded as an elevated and attractive role that was a stepping stone towards partnership. They embedded people management into promotion criteria for all management levels, from junior manager to partner. They built people management criteria into their external selection processes. Pay processes were changed to recognize people management, as well as client success. They then designed an integrated approach to people management (similar to the integrated talent management system described in Chapter 7), which linked all their training and development activities around a competency model. The managing partner and the executive committee were instrumental in promoting key messages around the importance of people management, and in backing the various initiatives. Much of the success of the culture change was down to the way it was built into the performance appraisal and reward programmes. Another factor of success was that, especially in communicating the programmes, the firm took pains to emphasize that people management skills were transferable to client relationships. This helped emphasize the importance of developing coaching skills. This firm has, since this culture change, consistently ranked as a leading organization for business performance, profitability and employee engagement.

This case study illustrates the importance of a coordinated approach where the organization's stance on its people is clear (vision) and where strategies and activities are designed so that they consistently align with this vision, rather than pull people in different directions.

'Vision' is aspirational and sets the tone and direction. An organization may convey in separate but related concepts the value it places on its people, how it will be perceived by customers, its ability to perform better than competitors; or it may encapsulate in a single concept what it aspires to achieve and to stand for. It must provide a focus for valuing talent.

'Values' express 'how we do things around here' and emphasize the behaviours that are important.

'Strategy' sets out the route to get from where we are to where we aspire to be, so we can determine what actions to take. This aligned approach gives us a 'shared understanding' of the business, and where it is going. Activities are then aligned to this broad strategic direction, and to the vision and values.

Standard Chartered provides an outstanding example of how a connected and coherent approach shapes the culture of the organization, underpins its values, guides its processes and activities and leads to business success.

When Dr Tim Miller joined Standard Chartered in 2000 as the then group head of HR, he established, at board level, principles of how to manage people across the organization. The first of these principles was that the bank would 'strive for excellence through strengths'. That is, it would be a place that would encourage people to develop and play to their strengths, not a place that focused on what individuals can't do. Moreover, at the heart of HR's role would be the aim to facilitate and strengthen the relationship between employee and manager as the key to driving high levels of engagement. These principles underpin the psychological contract between employees and the bank. They continue to guide how Standard Chartered is run, what the bank is like to work for, and how talent is identified, developed and deployed. These principles are formally encapsulated in Standard Chartered's commitment to stakeholders:

Our people: Helping our people to grow, enabling individuals to make a difference and teams to win.

Standard Chartered is structured into global businesses. Each has a global business head and business head of HR. The group HR function develops the bank's global talent processes and sets out the timetable of what needs to be done and by when so as to fit in with other processes, such as the business planning cycle. The processes themselves are owned by the business. This is achieved largely through a programme known as the Strategic People Agenda. Each global business presents an annual people agenda to Peter Sands, group CEO, and Tracy Clarke, group head of human resources and communications, setting out their people priorities on areas such as organization design, succession risks, critical talent pools including diversity, building technical and leadership capability and employee engagement. The business head and business head of HR report on the state of play in these areas, and discuss plans to address gaps or shortcomings, or put forward strategies to meet future business needs. They are challenged on each aspect of their agenda by the group CEO and group head of human resources and communications, who hold them accountable for achieving these goals and seeing these plans through to completion; in just the same way they are held accountable for other business results. In presenting their people agenda, business heads must show clear links between their agenda and global business goals. They are expected to make specific commitments regarding the development of talent and show their plans for talent movement. They are also asked to demonstrate explicitly how their talent moves will be aligned with the business strategy. For example, if they propose growth for their business, they are expected to show that they have the talent or can acquire the talent to support that growth.

These top-level conversations about the Strategic People Agenda set the tone, as well as the agenda. Business heads go back to their business units and engage their direct reports in their plans, and conversations around talent and performance are conducted right across the bank. Standard Chartered also actively manages its values and Miller believes 'values keep everything together'. Performance management takes this into account and people are expected to exhibit how they uphold the bank's values through the performance management process.

Standard Chartered employs over 75,000 people worldwide and has a very strong presence in Asia, Africa and the Middle East. The programme described here helps create a 'one bank' approach while leaving scope for local adaptation. In this way, it creates a clear way of doing things that guides and empowers but does not restrict. The business impact is significant as it leads to a consistent brand promise that is clear to all stakeholders, especially customers.

One of the most striking features of Standard Chartered's programme is how talent management is driven from the top through its Strategic People Agenda. Through this and the conversations it generates, the group CEO and group head of human resources and communications bring the bank's vision to life, they reinforce its values, and, together with the business heads and HR heads, set the broad strategic goals from which individual businesses and departments then plan their more local strategies.

In this next example, Carolyn Gray at GMG, working closely with GMG's group CEO, similarly uses influence and example from the top to set the tone and direction of the people agenda.

Gray has established a group-wide talent, development and succession programme for the top three management levels across GMG's different businesses. The rationale for this is to link activities on succession, learning and development so that the group achieves cohesion, consistency, economies of scale and greater synergy between each company, as well as opening wider career opportunities at the top.

Succession planning covering the top three senior management levels is driven from the top, and Gray and the group CEO discuss succession plans with each CEO every six months. Gray believes that if you are a CEO and you are required to regularly talk talent and development with the group chief executive and the HR director, this helps you develop a talent mindset. Although Gray concerns herself only with those on the succession plan at the top levels, she believes that when there is this level of interest and involvement from the top, people 'get it' and it filters down through each of the businesses, creating a talent mindset and sound practices. Ultimately, however, there is no 'must'.

Another of Gray's aims is for GMG to provide targeted development opportunities to enable people to work to their full potential, as well as meet its future needs. GMG has identified several long-term strategic strands for which it must now start building capability. These include capability for a changing world, leadership capability, and digital and marketing capability. The CEO of each of GMG's businesses must show to the GMG board how talent, learning and development activities relate to their business strategy, meet the highest quality standards and build this long-term capability.

Gray exercises control by measuring outputs. For example, if a business has a good talent strategy, she would expect more internal movement. Therefore she requires high-level reporting to show internal movement, rather than getting involved in the detail of what is done. In fact, Gray is not prescriptive with the businesses, which operate with a degree of autonomy and some of which are jointly owned with private equity. She sets out the model and how she will control results but believes there are many different ways to do things. In this, Gray sees herself as the enabler, setting out best practice and the minimum standards to be adhered to. Accountability for everything lies with the business, but she remains involved and provides support where needed.

As in Standard Chartered, Gray emphasizes the importance of conversations. She believes it is by talking things through that people develop a shared understanding of the business and its values. Moreover, conversations generate insights, which lead to creativity and innovation.

Gray has achieved a coherent talent and development strategy on a low budget, and can see that her strategy has created more career opportunities and enabled better cross-fertilization of ideas across the group. This in turn leads to a strengthening of the talent pipeline, especially the leadership pipeline.

Both these organizations have a talent management strategy that is closely aligned to the vision and values of the organization, and in both cases, the senior management team is actively engaged in shaping and supporting HR strategy as a whole, but specifically talent management strategy. The organizations recognize the pivotal role of people and have incorporated that into the core business model. The ultimate impact achieved by both is to create a clear brand promise that extends beyond the organization and helps all stakeholders know who they are and what they stand for, and be confident that they will deliver on this.

What are the implications of this for the organization whose CEO or senior management team is not on board with these ideas? Even if you do not have complete top level buy-in to this approach, creating a coordinated strategy that aligns with vision and values will help pull the organization in one direction, building consistency and familiarity in people's minds. Perhaps you will then find it has become 'how we do things around here'.

LEARNING POINTS

- Strategy is a connected series of activities that leads in a coherent direction and is powered by insights about the business and its markets. This fits with our view of talent management as being about focusing on the long term. It fits also with our view that talent management must generate insights so that people come away from the day to day and develop ideas and understanding that add value.

- Where talent management strategy is aligned with the organization's vision and values, this pulls the organization in a clear direction and creates a brand promise that is evident to all stakeholders. This leads ultimately to higher levels of employee engagement and customer satisfaction.

- One of the themes of this book is that talent management is not just about systems and processes but is also about a talent mindset, which recognizes the pivotal role of people in organizational success. Ideally, the organization's senior leaders have an important role in achieving a talent mindset across the organization, by incorporating that value into the core business model.

References and notes

1 Porter, M (1996) What is strategy?, *Harvard Business Review*, November–December

2 Campbell, A and Alexander, M (1997) What's wrong with strategy?, *Harvard Business Review*, November

3 Prahalad, C K and Hamel, G (1990) The core competence of the corporation, *Harvard Business Review*, May–June

4 Porter, M (1996) What is strategy?, *Harvard Business Review*, November–December

5 360-degree feedback is the term commonly used to describe feedback that comes from all around an employee. The person's manager, peers, employees and maybe clients are asked to give their views of the person's performance.

Developing the strategy

04

The ultimate purpose of talent management is to build organizational capability for the future in a way that ensures the organization retains flexibility in an uncertain world. This requires strategies for assessing, developing, deploying and engaging people.

A business has many strategies that interconnect and integrate with the overall business strategy. It is rather like nesting Russian dolls. You are presented with one doll. When you open this, you find another within, another within that and so on. Each conforms to the overall design but may have different painted features. Strategies for assessing, developing, deploying and engaging are connected through an overarching talent management strategy that aligns with organizational vision and values. The talent strategy is connected to the overall business strategy and is driven from the top.

A talent strategy shows the route to get from where you are to where you aspire to be and how to measure success along the way. This requires a clear understanding of your point of departure, and, at least, a pretty good idea of your destination. The reason you don't need to know this exactly is that strategy is about setting a direction for an organization to go in but the precise details are very likely to change as you pursue it. Strategy should therefore be flexible and able to accommodate some change and uncertainty.

To identify your points of departure and arrival requires identifying metrics that are important to your organization. These are indicators that will give you something measurable that correlates with success: for example, increased number of internal moves, availability of people to fill new roles or provide new skill sets, people who are identified as ready for the next move and are given the appropriate opportunity, and so on. Your strategy also requires communication, to involve as many people as possible, as well as gain insights into how people's efforts and behaviours impact on business performance.

This chapter will concentrate on the analysis you must do to identify these points of departure and arrival. This is a five-step process of analysis to enable you to identify what needs putting right and what will drive the business forward. I then offer guidance on developing the strategy, and finally look at how to measure progress.

Analysing your business

This five-step process consists of:

1 Interrogating employee engagement data.
2 Reviewing current practices.
3 Analysing business plans.
4 Identifying future capabilities.
5 Benchmarking with external practices.

Step 1: Interrogating employee engagement data

In discussing employee engagement in Chapter 2, we considered evidence of the link between engagement and performance and also identified that many of the indicators of successful talent management are also indicators of high levels of employee engagement. I would now like to consider how an understanding of current levels of employee engagement within the organization provides a datum point from which to measure change and also to help you to develop your talent strategy.

Some organizations are developing highly sophisticated uses of employee engagement data that are being used to make better strategic business decisions. This is generally being achieved by mapping the relationship between human capital practices and employee attitudes with customer attitudes, customer behaviour and revenue. Analysis of this kind can indicate how employees' attitudes to their jobs and company affect customer service and influence customer satisfaction. Sears, Roebuck and Co, for example, has mapped employee engagement data with customers' satisfaction about their shopping experience and the likelihood that they would return and would recommend Sears to friends and family.[1] The research showed that even small improvements in employee attitudes resulted in slightly higher levels of customer satisfaction, which in turn increased customer referrals and produced an increase in revenue growth.

McDonald's, Royal Bank of Scotland (RBS) and Standard Chartered are also leaders in the measurement of people and their relationship to business performance. McDonald's has analysed business results against the demographics of its stores and other data and found that, within a predominantly young workforce, customer satisfaction is more than 20 per cent higher in restaurants that employ one or more staff members over the age of 60 than it is in restaurants where none of the staff is over 50. This effect appears to arise through the presence of older workers helping to raise the performance and customer centredness of all staff, with the result that customer numbers, sales and satisfaction are increased. RBS has focused on establishing the linkage between improvement in people measures, such as engagement and employee satisfaction, and improvement in sales and customer service.[2] They have found that increasing engagement levels will also impact on business output measures. Standard Chartered, similarly, can demonstrate the relationship between levels of engagement and branch profitability. Moreover, Standard Chartered has also reported that in 2007 they found that branches with a statistically significant increase in levels of employee engagement (0.2 or more on a scale of five) had a 16 per cent higher profit margin growth than branches with decreased levels of employee engagement. This shows the benefit of continually improving engagement levels. Standard Chartered has continued to evolve its external reporting through its annual review and its sustainability review, which release significantly more data than in the past, and the bank is increasingly candid about the challenges it faces.

Sophisticated use of employee engagement data, such as described in these examples, that show how engaged people are and what entices them to leave the organization, go much further in aligning people management decisions with corporate objectives and measuring creation of shareholder value than is possible with the familiar measures of number of employees, turnover, etc. Perhaps it also moves HR away from a preoccupation about measuring its worth to focusing on measuring the business. If a new HR policy is designed to have an effect on people that will lead to a positive impact on business performance, then surely we should not waste time struggling to measure that original effect but should be measuring changes in business performance itself to find whether the policy has worked. Certainly employee data from different sources can be used to make business improvements, as well as helping to identify your talent management agenda and measure its success.

For example, a well-known transport company recently had technical problems that were compounded by poor customer service and communication with customers, leading to appallingly bad publicity. If this company has conducted an employee engagement survey it would be interesting to review the results. My guess is they would show low engagement in the customer-facing roles, poor internal communications and poor support from line managers, among other issues. Almost certainly analysis of such data before the calamity occurred would have highlighted serious problems and could have prevented huge financial losses through devastatingly bad publicity. A first step, therefore, in developing a talent strategy is to analyse the data generated by your employee engagement survey and any other data about employee perceptions. What do these tell you about practices that work well and those that don't?

Other sources of information include accounting and HR information systems, recruitment, service centre statistics, performance appraisal data, health and safety audits, succession plans, workforce plans, employee data including length of service, function, level, status and whether union or non-union. Your available budget is also a critical input, as it helps you know how to cut your cloth.

Do bear in mind the quality of data – how reliable they are and how easy to obtain – but examples of some common measures to look for are:

- staff turnover, by category, compared with industry norms and previous years: to identify problem areas, trends and patterns;

- internal promotions;

- absence levels;

- percentage of new hires leaving within the first 12 months;

- percentage of jobs / senior management roles filled from within;

- percentage of acceptances of job offers;

- speed to competence in new roles;

- percentage of people rated as high performers and their rate of promotion.

Also study external demographic data so you know how changes may affect your recruitment policies, and internal demographic data so you know how many people are likely to retire soon and so on.

Start by analysing data that are already available through existing management information systems but be willing to develop systems to collect new data if you believe that will provide useful insights. Sometimes data you want exist in places you have not looked, can be extracted from archived records or can be inferred from other indicators.

Interpretation is important, not least because people don't see what they don't want to see. A body with a public safety remit did not think it a problem that staff gave a low rating to 'It is safe to speak up' in an engagement survey. They allowed this to be obscured by high ratings given to other questions in that section. So interpretation demands picking up clues from different places and working out problems and questioning and, above all, an open mind.

Step 2: Reviewing current practices

In the previous chapter (see page 33) I set out common problems that arise in organizations that lack effective talent management. Use this as a benchmark or checklist against which to measure your processes and identify aspects of talent management that work well, and those that need improving or bringing into alignment. There are many different sources of information, such as completed performance appraisals, that you can use for this and that will yield powerful insights. Scrutinizing point-of-entry selection and promotion criteria, as well as the basis on which pay and bonus awards are allocated is also essential. These processes send messages about what the organization values and rewards. Every element of your talent management strategy must transmit consistent messages, otherwise it is the messages of the promotion and reward practices that will win through.

Conversations around the business will yield valuable insights: use them to seek people's views on how current practices help or hinder them, and to determine what will meet their needs and expectations. A theme of talent management is that practices should aim to support line managers in their people management responsibilities, especially to help them hold meaningful conversations about careers and performance that we have already identified as crucial to both talent management and employee engagement. 'How will this help line managers?' is a key question around which to examine your processes and design new ones so as to help line managers become coaches and talent managers.

Reviewing your practices in this way will help you identify practices to revise, and new ones to introduce. It should also help you prioritize and identify which to tackle first.

Step 3: Analysing business plans

A major attribute of talent management is that it balances projection into the future with unpredictability and it balances the need to build future organizational capability with the need to retain flexibility and adapt swiftly to change.

This requires people at all levels of the organization, but especially at the top, to project ahead and identify what looks certain, what the different options are, and how to retain flexibility. Any forward-planning information that is available should be examined at this stage. This may be written business plans, budgetary projections or workforce plans that look ahead at the key capabilities required to make business changes.

Step 4: Identifying future capabilities

This is about minding the capability gap. Identifying the gap between current organizational capabilities and what will be required in the future requires insight and conversations. Information that is on paper should be supplemented by conversations to generate these insights and challenge current thinking, so that constantly reviewing different future scenarios and constantly identifying how to do things differently become part of the agenda for people at all levels.

FIGURE 4.1   Mind the gap

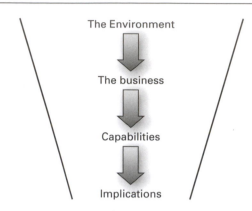

It can help to identify capabilities that will be required if people are led through a structured conversation that leads from business planning issues through to their implications on capabilities (see Figure 4.1).

The points to consider at this stage will vary from organization to organization but suggested questions are set out in Appendix A: Mind the gap. While not exhaustive, these are the most likely to be applicable to all businesses. The aim is to stimulate thinking across the business but also to collect information that will enable you to identify the gap between current and future organizational capability.

This thinking about future needs and capabilities is a shared responsibility where the front-end line manager's line manager may be involved and maybe the divisional director and the HR department. The point is to accept that whoever else may be involved, it is the role of each line manager and other individuals, especially professional and specialist staff, to be thinking forward, based on what they know of the organization's vision and plans and about the environment. Each must think about the capabilities that will be required within their sphere of influence, working to ensure these are developed so they are available when needed.

Line managers should also give thought to succession issues and identify or revise the capabilities required for certain roles and then consider who might develop these and how. In some circumstances, it may also be wise to identify who has scarce skills or knowledge and how they may pass these on and to whom.

This is not a one-off conversation. To help HR develop the talent strategy, it is a regular process that it should carry out with different people, and especially the top team, in the context of development and succession to keep these processes dynamic and relevant, and to stimulate people to keep identifying changes on the horizon. It should also be a conversation that helps you develop or revise your competency framework.

One of the main elements of talent management, emphasized in the previous chapter, is the importance of creating an integrated talent management system. This connects processes for assessing, developing and deploying people. The organization's competency (or capability, which is the approach I prefer) framework has a critical role in providing this connection. I explore the role of competency (capability) frameworks in Chapter 5.

Step 5: Benchmarking with external practices

Gathering external benchmarking data and bringing in new thinking and ideas from the outside should also form part of your analysis at this stage. What are your competitors doing? What is going on out there? What are some of the best practices? What are the pitfalls with each of these practices?

Benchmarking is the process of comparing business processes and performance metrics with other companies considered to be providing an industry standard benchmark or best practice. There are many sources of information that can be used for benchmarking, including sharing information across industry or sector groups, participating in research and surveys, conferences and networking. The last two are less reliable as people tend to talk up their experiences, and so my preference is with the first two.

An effective way of benchmarking, or bringing in ideas and thinking from the outside, is through the use of consultants. The recommendation here is to build solid, long-term relationships with external consultants, who can combine their outside knowledge and experience with understanding and insight into your business.

Some organizations carry out more formal benchmarking and compare their processes in detail with organizations they have identified as suitable comparators. I am not convinced this adds enough value to the methods suggested above to warrant the effort and expense.

ABC Engineering case study

This case study of ABC Engineering provides context to illustrate some of the ideas discussed so far. It describes steps taken to design a talent strategy, align it with vision, values and business strategy, and listen to the business to identify business challenges and future capabilities.

We took as our focus for this programme the business's stated values of openness, transparency and fairness. ABC's chief executive felt strongly that these, which were especially relevant to its external stakeholders, had to be applied internally to employees if they in turn were to feel committed to them and deliver them externally. He expressed this through two philosophies. The first was his 'Two dots' philosophy: he wanted everyone in the organization to have a dot representing where they are now in career terms, and one on the horizon, representing where they aspire to be. His other was 'Promises made, promises kept'; that is, he believed that the organization had made explicit and implicit promises to people at the time of their recruitment, which must be fulfilled. These philosophies, which he regularly referred to at formal occasions and in casual conversations, gave a clear message that he viewed individual development as important and therefore that each individual was important. This was, in effect, the 'people vision'.

Our first step in developing a talent management strategy was to spend a considerable amount of time 'listening to the business' – by talking to people, particularly at executive and senior management levels to understand where the business stood, what challenges lay ahead and what it needed to deliver. What does five years ahead look like, or 10 years, and how is it different from now? Until this point, ABC had relied heavily on achieving simply through assembling a high technical capability but, for the future, the target was to apply these skills to enable the 400 employees to shift up a gear to tackle the next phase of the business's strategic priorities. To do this, different behaviours would be required and would determine success.

Filling this behavioural gap was clearly a priority for our talent programme. These discussions were useful in addressing other issues like getting managers comfortable with the concept of development, having a common language and getting people to define the organization culture.

In these conversations, we also sought to find out which current practices worked well, which didn't, and what people needed to help them meet organizational goals and their own aspirations. Managers' concerns were around the need to have people who could perform the capabilities they knew would be needed for the future. Individuals expressed the need for more opportunities to build better relationships with their line managers. They wanted better-quality feedback and help to map their careers. There were a number of training programmes in place that were well regarded.

We also reviewed performance appraisal forms, aspirational interview forms and employee survey data. Taking these together, several problems became evident: line managers did not set goals properly, those they set were inconsistent, they had different ideas of what constituted high performance and they didn't give feedback properly.

From this preparatory work we were able to draw up a comprehensive talent strategy. We had a people vision and organizational values to keep referring to, we had identified the capability gap that we needed to fill to enable the organization to meet its future business challenges, and we had identified the initiatives and processes that needed to be improved or retained. We also had a clear indication that raising the quality of conversations between line managers and staff was a priority, and we were able to identify indicators from the employee survey to use to measure and track progress.

Our next step was to put in place an integrated talent management system that would enable us to achieve this strategy, and then involve the top team in setting the strategic direction. I will return to this case study, in ensuing chapters, to illustrate these next steps.

Before moving on, however, I would like to examine two other fairly typical scenarios. One is the organization that is in a period of rapid growth, whose focus must be on enabling speedy responses to recruiting, developing and deploying people. It may, therefore, be more appropriate to strengthen existing processes, or train more people to use them, rather than attempt to implement new ones that might involve a steep learning curve. Existing systems provide appropriate measures such as speed of filling vacancies, internal moves versus external hires, time to competency, percentage of leavers within the first 12 months, etc. The bottom line here is to make current processes work better and place the emphasis on conversations and relationships, without introducing new ideas.

The other scenario is where you may not have top-level support for a full talent strategy. We have discussed that it is nevertheless beneficial to draw up a talent strategy as a coherent, connected approach that will develop a picture in people's minds of what you are seeking to achieve, and this will influence behaviour. In such a situation, start by implementing practices that will meet the most important business needs.

Take the example of an academic institution that rarely appoints from within to senior positions. This issue is flagged at a board meeting and HR is charged with addressing it immediately. What are the underlying problems? An initial review shows that the organization is failing to differentiate levels of performance, provide appropriate feedback and development, or discuss people's aspirations with them. These are the first issues I would address, while also carrying out a five-step analysis and putting together a connected and coherent talent strategy to provide longer-term solutions. Since immediate action is required, my starting point would be to introduce a talent review and succession planning system to engage all line managers in conversations about people coming up through the organization and the development they should be offered. I would then ensure that development was provided as identified, supporting line managers in this where necessary. I would be targeting the people in the vulnerable group immediately, and providing appropriate development for all of them, which would include those identified as having potential to move to the next level. My next initiative would develop line managers' skills in discussing performance and careers, and I would possibly introduce line manager training and development based around a capability diagnostic tool such as I outline in Chapter 7. Incidentally, this would provide the foundation of an integrated talent management system that would connect all people processes and I would gradually implement this, and other aspects of my talent strategy. The key measure for these early stages would be the numbers applying for and being accepted for internal positions.

Designing your strategy

Having carried out your five-step analysis, the next task is to draw up the strategy, setting out its aims, the initiatives and processes you will put in place to meet these, and how progress will be measured. Your strategy should set out how to:

- align vision, values and current activities;
- mind the gap between current and future capabilities;
- select people who meet your future capabilities and fit with your cultural values;
- develop people in line with future business goals and capabilities;
- plan for succession;
- identify key measures of progress.

The component parts of a talent strategy – how you assess, develop, deploy and engage people – are examined in detail in the next chapter (see Appendices B and C for an overview).

Measuring success

We have discussed analysing data as the basis for action. Let us turn to using it to evaluate success after the event. Of course, some of the measures you will have identified as targets may still be appropriate but, as we saw earlier, circumstances may change, and your strategy must be flexible to allow for this. Moreover, different parts of your talent strategy will need to be evaluated along the way.

The difficulty of evaluating HR initiatives has been filling conference sessions for decades, which shows just how problematic this is. Looking at evaluating just a single intervention such as a training course or executive coaching helps us appreciate this. For some training programmes it is possible to set quantifiable objectives. For instance, if the goal is to improve an individual's presentation skills, then it is usually clear to the individual and their listeners whether this has happened. The problem arises when the goals are more complex. For example, suppose an objective is to enable someone to achieve a better strategic outlook. Their business area subsequently performs poorly: is this an indication of an unsuccessful programme? Not necessarily, the training may have led to better decisions but that does not guarantee improved business performance: long-established problems may have overwhelmed the improvements. Measurement based on larger samples will generally be much more reliable than a sample of one.

Following on from this we must recognize that the outcome of many training or coaching initiatives is intrinsically bound with what else is going on in the organization. Therefore any measurement of effectiveness must isolate the outcomes of the target initiative from these other factors. To illustrate this, suppose an individual's performance is potentially improved through training but shifting responsibilities within the organization frustrates their actual performance. This is the fault of neither the individual nor of the training.

What do you do with the results of formal, structured and expensive after-the-fact evaluations? Suppose you commissioned a formal evaluation of a coaching programme that concluded it had not worked. Oh! But why has it not worked? Can the defects be corrected? Would coaching be cost-effective if they can be corrected? Suddenly, having an answer reveals you are only at the foothills of an entire mountain range of questions, which are more difficult, costly and time-consuming to answer. Of course, knowing something is not working is a start to prevent pouring money into a black hole.

Another problematic issue is the concept of value. To evaluate the value of coaching can depend upon individual perception. What is of great value to one person is of little value to another. In evaluating an initiative, then, it is important to know 'from whose point of view'. As noted earlier, there are many audiences for evaluation results including the learners, their managers, *their* managers, senior executives, whoever implemented the initiative. For example, if someone becomes a more pleasant colleague as a result of coaching, that may mean nothing to one evaluator but be hugely worthwhile to another.

Because the perception of value varies, so do the purposes of evaluation. Moreover, the various audiences for evaluation frequently act as their own evaluators. Applying this line of thought to how to evaluate a talent management strategy, or parts of it, the following are important points to consider:

- the goals you set out to achieve and therefore what you want to measure;
- the purposes of the evaluation;
- how you will carry it out;
- the audiences for the results;
- the time frame to be employed;
- what you might do with the results.

The next issue is how to evaluate individual activities to see if they have produced the desired results. These can be evaluated on two levels. The first is considering the activity itself: for example, to identify if a coaching programme has achieved its aims. The second is to assess whether the activity has contributed to the achievement of strategic priorities. For example, are people staying longer with the organization because of training? You can examine existing data to estimate whether people's time to competency has improved and whether the level of contribution they make has improved after they undertook training at different stages. To do this often requires extrapolating data from different sources and identifying trends and patterns. For example, you find that an assessment centre programme used to recruit managers is well rated by participants and by the recruiting managers, which provides subjective data. You compare data from before and after the introduction of the programme on the level of job acceptances and also on the rate of successful recruits (perhaps comparing numbers leaving within 12 months). You may look at employee engagement survey data or performance management data that provide evidence specifically on the experiences of new recruits. From this or staff appraisal data it may be possible to estimate whether staff reached competence in new roles faster following the introduction of the assessment centre. Analyses of this kind depend on tracking operational figures, accounting data and employee engagement data over time.

Organizations such as Accenture and Saratoga have produced highly sophisticated models for measuring the return on investment (ROI) on training in particular. The Accenture ROI model shows a 353 per cent return on investment in training. Where the operating model for HR requires cross-charging its services to business units, much of this data should be easily obtainable. Accounting measures that can be matched with other data include: cost of labour, measures of health or staff turnover, absenteeism, average length of employee service, total training days per employee and levels of training investment as a proportion of employee costs.

To measure the effectiveness of elements of your talent management programme that relate to the leadership pipeline, you might analyse the internal reputation of the top team (from indicators on the engagement survey), the percentage of managers with necessary leadership capability or the percentage of managers ready to assume a greater role (from the succession plan).

Other talent management measures might be the number of people rated as high performers and tracking them through the system. Do they stay? Are they promoted? Are they promoted fast enough? And how do these percentages change over time? Staff turnover data can also give valuable information but must be accompanied by insights into why people are leaving, which may come through comparing data from different sources.

Employee engagement data should enable you to identify if you are succeeding in instilling a talent management mindset. For example, indicators about the effectiveness of line managers in carrying out meaningful conversations at performance review or in supporting people with their development or giving people stretching and challenging work will give you an indication of the impact of your talent strategy.

You may argue that analysis will never eliminate all extraneous factors: you may just have recruited a particularly outstanding group of managers, or the economic climate may have changed suddenly. Generally such events will be obvious and the analysis can be adjusted accordingly. You may argue that comparing data selected from different sources can be made to 'prove' whatever the analyst wants to. But this is true for any data analysis and it is up to the user of evidence or the reader of a report to consider the evidence and to decide whether it supports the conclusions: in this HR is no different from accounting or marketing or any other function.

The purposes of the evaluation and the audience for the results

An evaluation may produce valuable information for the person responsible for the talent management strategy but may be meaningless to others. For example, higher in the organization hierarchy it may be more important to identify key control measures, when those at the front line don't feel the need for this: their roles are not about control but about implementation. Researching into coaching a few years ago, I was struck by the number of HR directors who told me that they did not have time to worry about evaluating coaching and measuring its impact. They were happy to accept intuitive and anecdotal evidence to decide whether it was worthwhile. We saw earlier that Miller at Standard Chartered and Gray at GMG, both keep note of those identified as high performers. They would expect them to be promoted faster and would expect that to be reflected in their pay awards. Although individuals may be promoted because they have been flagged, if this risk can be addressed then measures of pay and time between promotions compared with peers are a good gauge of the success of the talent management strategy, as is having people available to fill roles when they are needed. These same measures might be important to those responsible for succession planning, but for different reasons, such as tracking how effectively line managers support high performers. Yet HR professionals lower in the hierarchy would have no direct interest in these measures. What is important, therefore, is for interested parties to identify the measures that matter to them. Intuitive and anecdotal evidence to measure success can be just as important as data. As Albert Einstein said, 'Not everything that can be counted counts, and not everything that counts can be counted.'

Communicating key achievements from the talent strategy around the organization is advisable. First, it gives recognition to those who have been involved. Second, it encourages continuing and perhaps increased participation: keeping the momentum going. Third, it communicates people and performance results, in the same way that you may communicate customer feedback or sales turnover.

Evaluation presents a conundrum. On the one hand, it is important to show that you are achieving results and obtaining value for money; but on the other hand, too much of it reeks of self-justification – and anyway, it is too easy to manipulate the evidence. I have witnessed programmes that have worked exceptionally well but someone with a personal interest in doing so has still found a reason to stop them. Similarly, I have known people lose their nerve, regardless of evidence of success. In HR, you are unlikely to get people jumping up and down with excitement to extol the virtues of your latest initiative. They will always have concerns: 'Can I do what is expected of me?', 'How will I have to change?', 'If I say it was excellent, will people expect too much of me?' There are, however, some answers to the measurement problem; they may seem to skirt the issue but that is the point: you will get more accurate and more usable answers by approaching the question indirectly:

1 Review progress by asking if this is taking you towards your goals.

2 Keep your nerve. If it feels right, it probably is – keep going. You are more likely to show demonstrable results over time than after the first step.

3 Build on what's already in place, rather than starting again. What you lose from imperfection is more than balanced by minimizing the change.

4 Don't 'pilot'. Organizations 'test the water', which signals to everyone that they do not have the courage to stand by their decision. It invites complaint. Develop something, think it through, run it, improve it, keep it going and keep trying to make it better.

5 Identify measures that will help you know what works well and what doesn't. Some of this may be anecdotal.

6 Identify indicators that show what you are contributing to business performance, such as people available to fill key jobs, people who are ready for promotion, etc. Identify what you need to keep control. Otherwise, use an employee survey to evaluate overall results of your talent strategy, rather than focus on individual initiatives.

LEARNING POINTS

- Develop your talent strategy by analysing your business. Use the five-step process: interrogate employee engagement and other data, review current practices and business plans, benchmark with external practices and identify future capability requirements.

- Importantly, engage people within the business in conversations about its needs and future challenges. These conversations (using the questions in Appendix A: Mind the gap) should be held regularly to stimulate thinking and generate insights, especially when planning development and succession.

- Identify the capability gap between where the organization is now and where it projects to be in the future and what systems to revise, discard or introduce.

- Line managers are critical to delivering talent management. Examine existing processes and design new ones with them in mind.

- This chapter introduced one of the main elements of talent management: an integrated system that connects processes for assessing, developing and deploying people. The organization's capability framework has a critical role in providing this connection.

- We often treat measurement of results as an end in itself. It is not. Its purpose is to inform and guide actions. Unfortunately, measuring results can distort them, and data can be used as a weapon by vested interests. Stand by your convictions, be bold, give it time, treat measurement with caution and focus on final goals not intermediate steps.

References

1 Rucci, A J, Kirn, S P and Quinn, R T (1998) The employee–customer profit chain at Sears, *Harvard Business Review*, January–February
2 Cheese, P, Thomas, R and Craig, E (2008) *The Talent-powered Organization*, Kogan Page, London

Assessment: Capabilities as the cornerstone of talent management

05

Selection decisions

Talent management comprises a range of activities that cover an individual's life cycle within the organization, from point of entry to point of departure.

FIGURE 5.1   Assessment

Figure 5.1 helps to give a sense of direction and sequence, but reality is complex and there are many linkages and much feedback. For example, as you develop people you also assess their progress in order to guide that development; deploying people in different roles also develops their skills; by developing them and then deploying them in challenging roles you also engage them; and by being engaged they will put more energy into their own development. The sequence may not always be followed: assessment may reveal capabilities that lead to an immediate change in deployment, either without development or in parallel with development plans.

Assessment has many uses and covers many purposes. It is a guide for making decisions on selection, succession and pay, but it is also the starting point for planning development, identifying strengths and deciding how and where these are best deployed.

Generally, line managers in the past formed assessments of people based on what they had achieved; but, in recent years, competencies have become widely used in selection and performance appraisal, as we have become more aware of the importance of those characteristics that give rise to results. Indeed, self-appraisal – where the individual analyses and assesses their own performance as the basis for discussion and action – has also become widespread. It helps generate a more constructive and open dialogue and, by definition, involves people in the process.

Most organizations have designed their objective-setting processes and competencies so that they are based upon agreed criteria, which individuals are aware of, and that assessment is not reliant upon single incidents that colour judgements. These are key principles for fair assessment.

Competencies are also used, in most organizations, to help people plan their development.

I start the discussion on assessment by exploring competencies, suggest how to get the best use out of them and propose alternative approaches, distinguishing between competencies and capabilities. Also in this chapter, I examine methods of assessment for making selection decisions and consider how to use these methods to create a new landscape that fits our changing times. I also start to explore the potential of an integrated talent management system. As the name suggests, this creates a joined-up management approach to assessment, development and deployment, using as its focus a single concept, such as the competency framework. This provides clarity and consistency and helps to create a shared understanding of the organization's success criteria and the capabilities that will be required in the future. An integrated system is the bedrock of talent management.

Competencies

The competencies approach was developed in the 1980s and 1990s as a way of providing the measurement of people. Two approaches took different paths at similar times. In the UK, the term used was competence (plural:

competences), which focused on training and development, specifying minimum standards for achievement of set tasks and activities, expressed in ways that were capable of observation and assessment. In the USA, Boyatzis coined the term 'competencies' as 'an underlying characteristic of an individual which is causally related to effective or superior performance in a job'.[1] These two different approaches can be summed up as being the difference between drivers of performance (US approach) and standards of performance (British approach). Recently, these approaches have tended to merge and a pragmatic route is to adopt both but to be clear on their use. As Roberts points out, the UK approach has limitations, especially for selection, since 'it places the emphasis on looking at people doing the work, and on the assumption that with sufficient effort they can be trained and developed to do the work'.[2] The US approach, on the other hand, can be helpful in making selection decisions because it is looking at the underlying characteristics which may not yet have had the opportunity to surface, and it is therefore concerned with potential rather than accomplishment. Nonetheless, a combination of the two is generally helpful, as assessment, whether for selection or development, should have the aim of identifying someone's potential as well as whether they can do the job.

The promise of the competencies approach is considerable. It offers a generic framework, which can be used for selection, development and succession planning. It provides a common language across an organization, it focuses people on the organization's success criteria, and it expresses the culture, values and strategic aspirations of an organization. This breadth is both an advantage and disadvantage.

Competencies, in fact, have many disadvantages and pitfalls. It is helpful to take stock of these, not least to know how to avoid them. The disadvantages are:

1 Competencies often amount to no more than wish lists, which are hard to argue against, as they express stereotypically desirable qualities.

2 Competencies that reflect organizational culture, such as 'creativity', 'innovation' and 'vision', tend also to be the most subtle and elusive of human qualities, which do not lend themselves to straightforward measurement or observation.

3 The concept of competency has a high degree of fluidity in its meaning and this is often reflected in the competency framework, which contains a mix of skills, knowledge, observable behaviours, intelligence, personal qualities, personality traits, organizational values, and skills required for the job, such as budgeting. This presents problems of both interpretation and measurement. Some competencies may mean different things to different people, and some may be hard to observe. Moreover, there is an argument that, in some roles, what the person does is more observable but less important than how they do it or what they know.

4   Competency frameworks vary considerably in length. Some
    psychologists argue that only eight competencies are required to
    predict performance in all managerial work (Baron *et al*[3]). But as lists
    of competencies get shorter and more generic, they also cease to describe
    the specifics of any particular role. In a 2008 report published by
    Incomes Data Services, the authors argued that a critical aspect of all
    frameworks is the degree of detail: 'If a framework is too general
    (containing only general statements about communication, team
    working, etc), it will not provide enough guidance either to employees
    of what is expected of them or to managers who have to assess their
    staff against these terms. If, on the other hand, it is too detailed, the
    entire process becomes excessively bureaucratic and time consuming
    and may lose credibility.'[4]
        They further observe that many managers and individuals find it
    hard to use the frameworks to help achieve goals. The reasons they
    give for this are that 'people don't see the benefit of the framework and
    aren't trained adequately; there aren't clear links to what the business
    is aiming to achieve and many frameworks are a mix of different
    concepts, which makes them unwieldy'.

5   There is often a tension between the extent to which competency lists
    describe current or future requirements.

6   Some writers have argued that competencies represent a form of control
    over individuals or are a way of cloning people. For example, historically
    loyalty and compliance characterized the individual's relationship
    with the organization. Competency frameworks have recently been
    used to move people away from this and towards entrepreneurial
    qualities. Other commentators suggest they impede creativity, as they
    generally capture the past and are therefore channelling people to
    focus on out-of-date requirements. This is especially problematic if
    competencies are linked to reward and recognition, which will
    encourage people to conform rather than innovate.

7   Competencies do not have the explanatory value of some
    psychological concepts such as intelligence or aptitude. They are,
    at best, convenient ways of describing and summarizing clusters of
    behaviour. This is especially evident when using competencies for
    development, because a low rating provides no explanation of why
    the individual is low in this area. The problem is compounded by
    competencies amalgamating traits, abilities and motivations. It is not
    clear whether the apparent lack of competence in the area is, for
    example, rooted in personality, or whether the individual was
    unwilling to display the behaviour. It is this lack of explanation and
    insight that causes 360-degree feedback, which usually reviews
    performance against competency descriptions, to end up at the
    bottom of a drawer. Without expert feedback and guidance, it is hard
    to know what to do with the information.

8 The way competencies are used tends to focus on what people can't do, which is not in keeping with our philosophy that talent management is about focusing on strengths. They also often underplay assessment of people for the way they mix and combine competencies. It is often how we mix them, combined with our personal qualities, that leads to success.

Nonetheless, the use of competencies is widespread. In 2005, my colleagues and I conducted a joint Scala/ACE survey across 93 UK organizations, each employing over 1,000 people, about their use of competencies. Over 77 per cent had been using them for more than three years.[5] This matches data from CIPD's 2007 survey into learning and development, which found that 66 per cent of respondents used competencies.[6] Those that did not tended to be smaller organizations employing fewer than 250 people.

My practical experience of competencies is that they are more effective than the problems listed above suggest. When they are well understood and used for more than one purpose, they add clarity to organizational success criteria and focus effort on the 'right' things. In fact, this was the case for 77 per cent of respondents to the Scala/ACE survey.[7] Most importantly, competencies are also a useful tool for line managers, as they open up areas of exploration, especially when individuals self-assess against the framework. In this way, they facilitate line managers' conversations with their employees about performance, learning and future roles. These conversations are essential to effective line management and relationship building. However, this requires mutual trust where the individual believes that a line manager will not take advantage of an honest self-assessment.

Self-assessment increases the efficacy of the process, as it encourages people to reflect on their performance, and they are then more likely to take ownership of how they can develop it. While insights into how personality may affect behaviour can be fascinating, you cannot change personality, but you can change your behaviour if you want to. Competencies, and especially 360-degree feedback programmes, often give people tips on how to fine-tune their behaviour, which can lead to performance improvements. Here again, the role of the line manager in holding conversations with their people to facilitate this reflection, and support development is important, though this role might also be taken by a coach or mentor.

Here are some examples of descriptions for a competency on communication:

- Facilitates and encourages discussion, ensuring that people listen to each other and exchange information.

- Emphasizes the positive points in a discussion and gives recognition to others for their ideas and participation.

These are observable behaviours that are appropriate for use in 360-degree feedback, as well as in a competency profile.

Competencies have also been beneficial in enabling businesses to implement change programmes, as they can be a highly effective way of emphasizing new organizational success criteria. In this way, they are as much about planning and communication as they are about control and direction, thus avoiding the disadvantages of creating conformity or coercion.

In summary, competencies have advantages and disadvantages but they are widely used. Where they are understood and used well, there is a strong argument for developing them, paying attention to avoid their disadvantages, and crafting them to meet the requirements of talent management. The following are some processes and ideas for maximizing the benefits of competencies.

Classification of competencies

The following classification of competencies, developed by Roberts, differentiates types of competencies. He suggests that the language of the framework is not important, rather the 'classification is the critical element since it facilitates a practical balanced system for managing competencies'.[8] He suggests that a competency framework should be grouped into the following 'clusters':

1 *Natural.* These would be our innate or underlying traits. Thus, they often relate to the 'big five' dimensions of personality. (In contemporary psychology, the 'big five' factors of personality are five broad domains or dimensions of personality, which have been scientifically discovered to define human personality. They capture most of the differences we observe between each other's personality. They are also deemed to be relatively stable over time.) These dimensions are extraversion/introversion, emotional stability, agreeableness, conscientiousness, and openness to experience. They may include competencies such as judgement or resilience. The possession of innate qualities does not guarantee the person will successfully apply their talents, but selecting people with the raw ingredients is an essential prerequisite. Attempting to train or artificially create such natural talent is unrealistic.

2 *Acquired.* These competencies express the knowledge and skills that are developed through study or experience (eg professional knowledge, business awareness).

3 *Adapting.* This is the critical set that enables the individual to succeed in their work environment. All too often people are successful in one role but fail to maintain this when they change job. This can be as true of people who are highly rated but then fail to make the transition to a new department or organization, as of people being promoted. Whether coming to terms with a different culture, a different operating

environment or a different set of priorities or demands, success will flow from the ability of the individual to adapt their natural talents and acquired knowledge to current circumstances, (eg adaptability, learning, open to new ideas, innovativeness, exceeding stakeholders' expectations.) Adapting competencies should be used as the focus for development activities, since this is what Roberts describes as 'the accelerator, which the person uses to apply his or her natural abilities and knowledge or experience'.[9] Adaptation competencies affect a range of behaviours from innovation to regulation and indeed cultural fit, commitment to corporate goals, team working and decision making. Since this is the point at which the person 'chooses' whether to apply their natural or acquired competencies, it is the area where development activities can have the greatest leverage in enhancing performance.

4 *Performing*. Performing competencies are already the focus of much attention as the observable behaviours and evidence of performance. An example is: 'Knows who the customers are, ensuring that they receive an accurate and prompt service by taking responsibility for making things happen.' It is the area most frequently covered in competency frameworks. These are useful as the basis for evaluating performance and can provide a common language for objective appraisal and feedback.

Roberts groups competencies into these clusters instead of having a single list that can be a mix of personal qualities, observable behaviours, etc. He suggests that where an organization has a list, to put those that are really about personal qualities into the natural group; those that concern what you know into the acquired group; those that are about learning and adapting to change into the adapting group. Finally, the performing competencies are observable behaviours in the way you work, such as giving customer service. He says there is a flow. The starting point is your natural competencies, which are to do with your personality and are unchangeable. Acquired competencies are what you have learned. You work from both of these to achieve results, but how effectively you use them depends on how effectively you adapt to change, learn new things, etc, which is the adapting cluster. When you group competencies in this way it is clearer how to assess them. For instance, personality testing can identify personal qualities, you can test numeracy (acquired) or you can talk about customer service or budgeting (performing). You can also test adapting through personality or other profiling tools.

A framework showing how these clusters fit together is shown in Figure 5.2. It also shows the flow between competencies: natural and acquired competencies are turned into successful performance by the use of adapting competencies.

FIGURE 5.2   Roberts's competencies framework

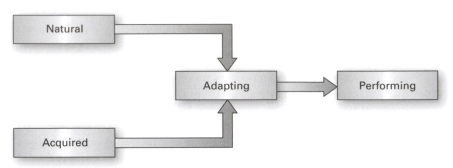

From Roberts, G (1997) *Recruitment and Selection: a competency approach*, with the permission of the publisher, Chartered Institute of Personnel and Development, London (www.cipd.co.uk)

This structure provides an identifiable framework of cause and effect. It makes the management of competencies clearer and it is easier to separate out observable from non-observable competencies. It is then possible to identify appropriate assessment methods for each of the different clusters. This is valuable for selection, development and career planning.

In selection, this approach enables the candidate specification to be divided into components that relate to these clusters so that a complete picture can be built, component by component. As Roberts points out, this 'avoids the difficulties of whole-picture assessments, in which selectors are trying to make an overall judgement of a candidate but are not able to specify clearly the elements where they believe the candidate may or may not fit the requirements of the role'.[10]

Turning to the role of competencies in creating an integrated talent management system, it will be helpful to clarify the difference between competencies and capabilities, as I use them here.

The dictionary definitions of the two terms show they share one meaning: 'the ability to do something'.[11] But capability has two other meanings: 'talent that could be developed – an ability or characteristic that has potential for development'; and 'potential for use – the potential to be used for a particular purpose or treated in a particular manner'.

Hence the term 'capabilities' is useful to convey the message that these are characteristics for development and not ones that either the individual or the organization collectively is expected to have already mastered or demonstrated. Moreover, as we have already determined, competencies as they are defined by organizations do not just express things people can do, but include a mix of other attributes such as organizational values, areas of knowledge, technical abilities and so on. By using the term 'capability', we can narrow the definition to those things a person can do, either because they have the 'natural' traits or because they have the ability to adapt and use the knowledge and experience they have acquired. The term therefore covers the behaviours that fall within the natural and adapting clusters and so suits my purposes well. I will use it throughout this book to specifically refer to an integrated system.

Integrated system of talent management

One of the benefits of extracting and using behavioural capabilities from the broader mix of competencies is the practical application it offers for a system of integrated talent management.

The first step is to follow the process I set out in Chapter 4, and engage people around the organization in conversations that stimulate them to identify future business challenges and the capabilities required to achieve these.

At this stage, you may wish to identify technical and professional capabilities, as well as behavioural ones (these would fall within the acquired and performing clusters on Roberts's framework) and so should use other job analysis techniques for this. These techniques include bringing together people who understand what is involved in the roles to analyse them and identify the key capabilities underpinning successful performance. Another, critical-incident interviews, involves interviewing job holders and their managers to identify and analyse specific tasks that form a critical part of the role. Repertory grid is one tool for analysing differences in performance and drawing out the capabilities that cause them. Each of the techniques referred to above has advantages and disadvantages and the ideal approach is to use a range so that the end result is comprehensive and balanced.

What is important is to pull out from your discussions across the business the behavioural capabilities that fall within the natural and adapting clusters and use them to create an integrated system. You do this by relating a range of HR processes to these critical capabilities. So you use them for assessment, development and deployment. You recruit people against them, use them for performance appraisal and for assessing development needs, planning development and measuring progress. You design learning materials around them, use an understanding of people's capabilities to help identify whom to deploy where, and understanding of capability gaps to train or develop people to fill them.

These capabilities must include those that will enable you to keep pace with the shift to an innovation-based economy, where success comes not just from what you know, but how you use that to imagine new ways to get work done, solve problems and create new knowledge. There are several behavioural capabilities that are universally important to 'new world' organizations: problem solving, handling conflict, building relationships, adapting, learning and being open to new ideas. Capabilities related to people management are essential for those in roles where they manage others.

Figure 5.4 below is an example of an integrated talent management system. It shows the link between different people processes and the organization's capability framework, which in turn links to future business challenges.

FIGURE 5.4

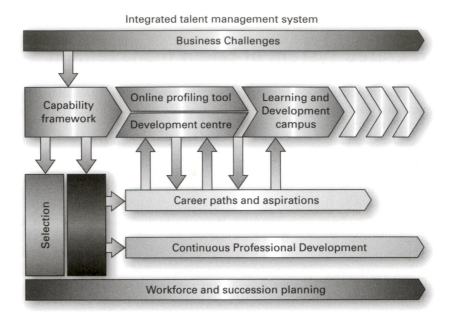

Integrated talent management system

I will describe an integrated system in detail in Chapter 7. For now, I wish to discuss assessment for selection, and show the role of these capabilities in this context.

Taking risk by reducing risk

Organizations are often risk averse when it comes to job appointments. A sales manager is sought to fill a sales manager vacancy. Not only does such an outlook restrict the available candidate pool, it is also becoming structurally impossible. Let's consider these points for a moment. The skills shortages that first gave rise to the 'War for Talent' are still there, even though in some areas they eased slightly as a result of the recession. Demographic changes mean the workforce is getting older, not younger. Better health combined with worse pensions is creating a large pool of workers who years ago would have already retired. As a result of the recession, a generation of school leavers and graduates may have been denied the usual training posts, and women returners may have extended their period out of work. Increasing numbers of people are not following traditional career paths, for a whole host of reasons. The pace of change rapidly makes some skill sets obsolete and creates others not previously on the radar. And then add to this mix people's expectations. Since the demise of the 'job for life' mentality, the psychological contract has changed. People aren't content to progress slowly, they want development, challenge and opportunity, and they want to be able to see what the future holds for them in the organization. Not everyone is ambitious, but most people recognize that they need to keep pace with change in the environment, and they expect the organization to support this.

It has always been rare that the ideal candidate fully meeting the requirements of the role steps forward for a vacancy, especially for 'point of entry recruitment'. This will become even less likely in the future. It is not my aim here to set out a 'how to' guide of recruitment and selection. There is much research and guidance available already. Rather, my aim is to raise the points that are crucial to talent management, especially to creating a talent mindset:

- Assessment criteria should seek to ascertain if the person can do the job, if they fit with the cultural values of the team they would join and of the wider organization, if they can cope with the change inherent in the job, and if they might fit with a range of job roles, especially those on the horizon. For the recruitment and selection of managers in particular, emphasis needs to be placed on the capability dimensions of change, ambiguity and uncertainty, rather than of order and predictability. The capabilities discussed earlier should be able to serve this purpose.

- 'Past performance is the best predictor of future performance' has long been the basis of most recruitment and selection. Certainly, selection decisions should take past performance into the mix. It is, however, worth bearing in mind that some people may not yet have had the opportunity to use certain skills or behaviours. Moreover, people are affected by the system in which they operate, the way they are managed, and other factors. That one environment brought out certain behaviours is no guarantee that this will be the case again. Furthermore, as Roberts argues, 'overemphasis on observable behaviour ignores the personal characteristics necessary for success'.[12] This is especially so as the capability dimensions that indicate whether the person can cope with the change inherent in the job fall within the natural cluster, that is, innate qualities that cannot easily be trained. However, while personality and psychometric testing may identify whether the person possesses these raw ingredients, it does not guarantee they will successfully apply their talents. For example, personality testing may reveal someone as low on certain people skills, but the person may nonetheless be an outstanding line manager, having learned these behaviours, perhaps from good role models or from training. The reverse may be equally true.

So what is the way through these apparent contradictions? I offer here some pointers:

- Identify the critical capabilities and the different ways they can be assessed using Roberts's framework. Make sure that selectors are thoroughly familiar with using these capabilities as assessment criteria. A common fault with interviews and assessment centres is that selectors understand the capabilities, but are unable to assess the candidates' responses against them.

- Personality and psychometric testing are widely used. As long as data from such instruments are treated as tentative and inferential, they are helpful to open up areas of exploration with candidates at interview.

- Even more advantages can be achieved through assessment centres. These assist the whole process by giving candidates experience of parts of a job, giving them the possibility of getting to know the organization, while giving selectors the opportunity to assess existing performance and predict potential. The term 'assessment centre' refers to a technique rather than a place and a centre may be run just for an individual or for several candidates at any one time. The assessment centre approach combines a range of techniques – interviews, psychometric tests, exercises, role plays and simulations – to give the fullest possible picture of a candidate. It is the use of simulations that distinguishes assessment centres from other selection techniques, by making it possible to observe the person 'at work'. Assessment centres must be professionally run, fair, ethical, reflect the ethos of the organization, use skilled and trained assessors, assess the key organizational capabilities, and give sensitive and supportive feedback to candidates afterwards. They should reflect the reality of the job and the organization. They are especially valuable for 'new world' recruitment, as a well-structured centre can enable recruiters to focus on the new capability dimensions of change, while also assessing cognitive ability and job-specific capabilities. Assessment centres produce a vast range of information about the candidate, gained through different processes and from different sources. This is especially helpful when it comes to assessing older workers and others who may previously have been doing something different, or those who have not followed traditional career paths, or younger workers with little work experience and those for whom the new role represents a big leap forward. This means they are helpful in enabling organizations to take a risk with someone.

As with all selection methods, assessment centres are not foolproof. Fincham and Rhodes point out that assessment centres 'very often do not deliver on their promise or the considerable resources invested in running them'.[13] The reasons they cite for this are concerned with the difficulty of rating people, especially doing so consistently. Fincham and Rhodes also believe that assessors tend to mark exercises rather than the dimension the exercises are supposed to be measuring.[14] These problems, however, are also often present in interviewing. Ensuring observers are well trained and have opportunity to build their skills helps overcome these problems. Designing assessment centres so that they produce evidence of a candidate's behaviour from a multitude of sources also reduces these problems, by providing corroborative evidence.

Assessment centres enable you to widen your candidate pool, but being less risk averse also requires different attitudes and understanding on the part of recruiting managers, and a more open-minded approach to drawing up job and candidate specifications. It also requires a talent mindset, where line managers go deeper than education and track record and seek to understand someone's abilities and aspirations, and are prepared to support them while they rise to new challenges. Training line managers and using them as observers on assessment centres is a valuable way of giving line managers this understanding. This also reaps other benefits, as it gives them a better understanding of the organization's capabilities and significantly develops their skills of giving feedback.

An important part of being able to take a risk with someone, however, is how much the person wants the opportunity. This brings me to my next point, that enabling people to self-select is vital.

Make point of entry selection a collaborative endeavour

With any selection both parties have to make a decision. From my experience, when new recruits fail, a common reason is that they had not fully understood what the job entailed, or perhaps this had not been put across to them well enough. Giving people information to help them make a decision may sound obvious, but rarely happens in practice.

The candidate is the best placed of everyone in the recruitment process to assess whether they can do the job, whether it fits their aspirations, and whether they will fit in to the team and the organization. Moreover, from my experience as an interviewer, you are able to gain better-quality information from people who have had an opportunity to find out about the job and the company beforehand, and this gives you more to go on when assessing their suitability. New technologies enable organizations to provide much better information than ever before. Podcasts, videos, possibilities to interact, social networking opportunities with people the candidate will be working with are just some of the ways of providing information to candidates to enable them to self-select.

Bekaert case study

Bekaert is a global market leader in drawn steel-wire products and applications and a technological leader in its core competences: advanced metal transformation and advanced materials and coatings. Founded in 1880, Bekaert is a global company with headquarters in Belgium, customers in 120 countries, 23,000 employees worldwide and combined sales in excess of 3 billion euros.

Worldwide, Bekaert has around 2,000 managers. Company policy is to arrange a formal assessment each time they recruit a manager externally. Their main aim is to get a second opinion but this process also enables them to achieve global consistency in their hiring policy. The assessment centre is run as the final stage of the selection process, and is offered only to the preferred candidate, not the other shortlisted contenders. Generally, the assessment centre is the final stage of the selection process. The earlier stages are interviews held by the line manager, the line manager's line manager, and the HR manager and also psychometric testing. Candidates from outside Belgium generally visit the Belgian headquarters, where they have the opportunity to meet the director responsible at HQ level for the unit they are to join.

Neil Purshouse, who is HR manager based in Belgium of Bekaert's Global Wire business, explains that they have 'built a strong relationship and rapport' with an external consultancy that has been running their assessment programmes for some years and both parties know each other well. In this way, the consultants have developed an understanding of Bekaert that enables them to identify cultural and organizational fit from an objective, external perspective and, importantly, to provide consistency.

Purshouse believes that it is immensely valuable to have this different perspective and additional information. The process also provides information about potential that is less easy to identify through interviews. Each candidate is discussed with the consultants, who also provide a detailed, written report. Bekaert seeks a recommendation from them as an important input into the final hiring decision but they do not always follow this. While the consultants' understanding of Bekaert is important, their main task is to assess candidates against the behavioural competency profile for the role. Purshouse values this professional assessment against the company's competences but recognizes that there may be circumstances when a candidate brings other skills and qualities or, perhaps, experience that might compensate for a failure to meet competences to the level required. He also believes it is important that line managers do not see these assessments as relieving them of responsibility for exercising judgement and making a decision.

In Purshouse's view, another benefit of the assessment centre process is that it is a valuable input that the line manager can use to plan induction and development. Within a short time of a new employee starting, Purshouse arranges a debrief attended by the new recruit, the line manager and Purshouse. They discuss the person's report and identify development plans, which helps the line manager and new recruit establish the basis on which they will work together. Purshouse believes this meeting is critical to ensuring the assessment is followed up.

The new recruit has a four-month development review with their line manager and after six months has a review with the HR manager to discuss progress and to discuss whether the person's development needs were followed through.

Historically, Bekaert recruited the brightest from Belgium's universities, though one of its aims now is to encourage greater diversity among employees to match its global reach. It is achieving this partly by extending its range of recruitment sources, such as the minorities recruitment fair held in London, to widen its candidate pool. This assessment centre programme then helps ensure that different perspectives are brought into the recruitment process, so that people are recruited on the basis of whether or not they meet job requirements and not on any other criteria. Moreover, Bekaert aims for a 'one company' global approach but recognizes the importance of allowing people scope to adapt to local culture and local needs, as well as to give autonomy and independence.

The assessment centre programme is a way of achieving these aims. For example, at Scala, as UK partners of the Belgian consultancy CPM, we ran an assessment centre programme for the recruitment of a director in the UK. We were thoroughly briefed on the role, the company, the competency profile, the reporting procedure and details of previous assessment centre programmes. The requirement was for us to work to the same competency profile and to produce a report consistent with the global reports. Otherwise, as long as we included a range of methods and instruments, how we carried out the assessment centre was left to us.

The alignment that Bekaert achieves through its vision, values, strategies and HR practices enabled us to understand Bekaert, its competencies and its requirements more easily than we generally find with other organizations where these are not as well aligned.

This clarity, as well as the level of effort and the investment Bekaert puts into the recruitment process, enables Bekaert to achieve highly satisfactory levels of success, especially with recruits who remain with the company for the long term. Purshouse also believes it results in faster induction. As the process is well developed, assessments are generally carried out quickly and do not cause delays to decision making, which are more likely to occur in organizations where there is less clarity over job requirements and cultural fit. In these cases, there is often a tendency to compare candidates with each other, which means seeing additional candidates and perhaps having more people involved in the process.

Bekaert does not just use this assessment centre approach for external recruitment. Development centres using similar approaches are also run for existing staff, generally to enable individuals to develop a career plan, to identify their next career move or to obtain an independent perspective on potential.

LEARNING POINTS

- Assessment criteria should include capabilities that are essential for success in today's environment: solving problems, creating new knowledge, learning, adapting, being open to new ideas, handling conflict and managing relationships.

- Increasingly people are not following traditional career paths. Different and broader methods to assess if someone has the transferable skills or the innate qualities for the role are required, and assessment centres can be beneficial for this.

- Assessment centres are also beneficial for achieving global consistency, as well as facilitating induction and initial development. Assessment centres bring robustness to the selection process, and open areas for exploration with the candidate.

- Giving people ample information and possibility for interaction so that they are able to self-select for jobs is valuable and is facilitated by the growth in technological solutions.

References

1 Boyatzis, R E (1982) *The Competent Manager: a model for effective performance*, Wiley, Chichester
2 Roberts, G (1999) *Recruitment and Selection: a competency approach*, CIPD, London
3 Baron, H, Bartram, D and Kurz, R (2003) The Great Eight framework for validation research, *Proceedings of the Occupational Psychology conference*, British Psychological Society, Leicester
4 Incomes Data Services (2008) *Competency frameworks*, HR studies, 865, IDS, London
5 http://www.thescalagroup.co.uk/resources1.html
6 Learning and development survey 2007: http://www.cipd.co.uk/subjects/lrnanddev/general/_lrndvsrv07.htm
7 http://www.thescalagroup.co.uk/resources1.html
8 Roberts, G (1999) *Recruitment and Selection: a competency approach*, CIPD, London
9 *ibid*
10 *ibid*
11 *Encarta World English Dictionary* (1999), Bloomsbury Publishing, London
12 Roberts, G (1999) *Recruitment and Selection: a competency approach*, CIPD, London
13 Fincham, R and Rhodes, P (2005) *Principles of Organizational Behaviour*, 4th edn, Oxford University Press, Oxford
14 *ibid*

Assessment: Performance management and reward

06

FIGURE 6.1   Assessment

Talent
Management

Engage Deploy Develop Assess

Assess Develop Deploy Engage

Talent management is as much about managing the performance of the individual as it is about developing potential; and since both performance appraisal and reward are key components of managing performance, this chapter highlights ways in which they integrate with and reinforce an inclusive approach to talent management. It also considers 360-degree feedback, which is increasingly being used by organizations as part of performance appraisal, though it is also an effective development tool.

Cultural messages

Performance appraisal and reward policies send out strong messages to people about what the organization values and what it sees as its priorities. The basis on which pay and bonus awards are allocated and on which people are promoted, especially to management roles, puts across vital messages about what is really important to the organization. As discussed in an earlier chapter, every element of your talent management strategy must transmit consistent messages, otherwise it is the messages of the promotion and reward practices that win through. If you wish the organization to value talent, then this must be rewarded and recognized through performance appraisal, pay and promotion, as well as more subtly by the behaviour of the people at the top. Similarly, it is vital to pay attention to how individual achievement is rewarded compared to team achievement. As technology makes it increasingly easier for us to interconnect, so it becomes more important for us to do so. In other words, collaboration and teamwork are becoming more critical and must also be built into reward programmes where appropriate.

Performance goals

Performance objectives describe something to be accomplished – a point to be aimed at. They are designed to support business objectives and are normally intended to bring about change rather than just modest one-off individual improvement, but they are also often part of a policy to create continuous improvement. They should focus on the key aspects of the job and not focus on one area at the expense of the others. The integration of objectives up, down and across the organization is important in order to achieve a shared understanding of performance requirements. Whether you call them goals, objectives or targets, setting them can be difficult. It is hard to make them measurable, keep them current, and to achieve consistency across the organization, especially when it comes to identifying who has met their objectives or targets and who has exceeded them.

The appraisal process operates hand in hand with goal setting and when designing that it is helpful to consider broad questions such as:

- Are targets extracted from the business plan?
- Are they new or special things for someone to achieve over the next year?
- Do they cover the day-to-day responsibilities of someone's role?

These are important questions to address, as often people's objectives and consequently their overall appraisal omit their continuing day-to-day responsibilities, yet these might be vital to organizational performance.

Achieving a balance between recognizing and rewarding continuing responsibilities and new (targeted) ones is important to talent management. There is no one answer to this, and the balance will vary for each role and individual.

It can be helpful for line managers to work through the following thought sequence when they are setting objectives:

- What are the most important things the person does?
- Why are these things important?
- What do you want the person to achieve in each of these areas?
- How does this fit with your own plans for yourself and your department?
- How does this fit with organization-wide objectives?
- What will happen if these results are not achieved?
- What are the limitations and constraints?
- Can this be done with the resources you have?
- What time frame is realistic?
- Has anyone else done this successfully?
- Do we need to revisit priorities to make this happen?
- What do you want this person to stop, start or continue doing?
- How does this person need to interact with others?
- Who might depend on this person or on whom might this person depend to be able to achieve the desired results?

An attribute of talent management is the notion of development by experience, and performance objectives should include responsibilities, projects, etc that will enable people to develop and move towards their career aspirations, preferably through opportunities that offer accelerated development. So the targets are not just linked to advancing business objectives but also have a role in stretching and developing the individual, which will bring indirect business benefits.

Do targets cover 'soft' objectives? In the new world organization, coaching their people and being an effective talent manager must be a required skill for all line managers. This can be expressed in a competency profile but should it also be transferred into a hard objective? Yes, because importantly this gives line managers accountability for talent management. However, to be effective, it requires alignment with vision and values. Bekaert has achieved this alignment, and being a talent manager is seen as 'how we do things around here' and is incorporated into appraisals.

Where alignment is lacking, such a question may be treated with cynicism. In this case, progress towards it in stages, starting by incorporating it in your competency profile and providing appropriate support and training for line managers.

Differentiating performance

There is increasing evidence to show that where companies concentrate on differentiating top performers from those at the bottom, this has the effect of raising levels of achievement among all staff. Identifying and recognizing high performers is wholly compatible with the notion of an inclusive approach. Inclusive talent management means something for everyone, not just a few. It means recognizing different levels of contribution, and providing appropriate development, experience and support. Differentiating top performers is especially important in the new world organization where the emphasis needs to be on collaboration, not competition. In the old organizational model, competition often drove standards of performance. The emphasis now on collaboration doesn't mean reducing everything to the lowest common denominator, but raising it to the highest. This means line managers must be fair and consistent about what differentiates performance levels. There are various ways in which staff performance can be differentiated. Examples include comparing one person with another, absolute performance versus relative value, such as the apportioning of bonus payments as discussed in the section below on reward, and by assessing past performance.

Person-to-person methods are primarily achieved through appraisal ratings and forced ranking.

Those who disapprove of performance appraisal ratings that link directly to pay, whether this is a performance award or a bonus, believe it detracts from focused discussion on the task of giving feedback on performance and identifying development needs. Moreover, when there is a direct link to pay there is a danger that this tends to create a limited, bureaucratic approach and turns appraisal into a pay negotiation. Another inherent problem of awarding performance ratings linked to objectives is that this is a short-term and often arbitrary approach linked to the financial or the pay year. The year end may not be the best time to assess whether the objective has been achieved. This is especially the case with people at the upper end of the organization's hierarchy, where you expect and need the impact to be long term.

Some points in favour of ratings are that they give an important macrolevel view of performance and also provide valuable management information. Addressing the problem of turning the discussion into a pay negotiation, the performance appraisal rating may only be one input into the pay decision, the others being cost of living and any considerations of internal or external relativities. This takes the heat off the link with pay in the appraisal meeting. Realistically, the spectre of appraisal affecting pay is always there, as someone whose appraisal is just average and who has not achieved all their objectives is unlikely to expect the top-performance pay award.

There is no clear answer as to whether appraisal ratings are good or bad. This depends on a host of variables such as the competence of line managers, levels of trust, organizational culture and the detailed operation of the pay-and-reward process. I have come across instances where line managers are inconsistent across the company in assigning ratings and, in these circumstances, I do not recommend a direct link to pay. On the other hand, introducing ratings can help to achieve that consistency. To make this effective requires bringing line managers of the division or department together to discuss performance and potential of their staff.

An argument often levelled against performance appraisal systems is that they allow managers to inflate ratings and award superior ratings to all. Forced ranking was developed to overcome this problem, as it requires a certain percentage (often 10 to 20 per cent) to be in the top ranking and a similar percentage (often 10 per cent) of people to be in the bottom rank, from where they are usually shown the door. In my view, this is incompatible with my talent management approach, which is about raising performance levels generally and dealing with poor performance immediately and at source. First, ranking is an easy way out of discussing and managing poor performance for line managers who are able to say, 'I would have given you X but I couldn't because of forced ranking.' Second, it requires some people to be allocated to the bottom rank. Most line managers dislike forced ranking, feeling it does not help them manage staff as they wish. They especially dislike having to identify that bottom tranche, finding it hard to raise performance levels of steady and valuable contributors by setting them new or more challenging targets, as these people fear suddenly finding themselves in that bottom tranche. The very act of creating a 'poor performers' category limits people's willingness to try new things and take risks, and therefore limits the performance of satisfactory performers. Third, making it a secret process goes against the ethos of open and honest discussions about performance, which we encourage. Secrecy anyway, especially if records are kept, contravenes data protection legislation, which requires employees to be able to access information held about them. Finally, forced ranking discussions can degenerate into battles among managers who manipulate the system to favour certain employees.

Those in favour of forced ranking generally argue that it allows more accurate cross-department comparisons and that it forces managers to think in greater depth about the quality of talent in their team than conventional performance appraisal systems typically require. They also argue that it forces line managers to describe and verbalize their assessments about people and this provides a good indicator of a critical aspect of the managers' leadership ability. My own view is to try and achieve these benefits by bringing line managers together with their peers to discuss performance levels but to avoid forced ranking, which is problematic unless your line managers are highly skilled. On the whole, I believe it is effective to keep a link between appraisals and pay, but to separate discussions about development.

Competencies and values

Performance targets and their appraisal also relate to competencies (I revert to this term temporarily to refer to common practice) and values. Even though reviewing performance against competencies is standard procedure for most organizations, it nonetheless tends to be problematic. First, many organizations require people to be assessed against the full competency profile. This is bureaucratic and unpopular and leads either to long, laborious appraisals or to the opposite: a quick rush through ticking all the boxes. Second, there is sometimes confusion between competencies and values. Third, competency assessments often add to the conflict between line manager and appraisee over appraisal ratings. There is, of course, an irony here as the whole idea of competencies is to emphasize that how you achieve results is as important as what you achieve. It should follow, therefore, that if someone met their sales targets but failed to share information or support a colleague, and so did not uphold the teamwork competency, this should be reflected in their competency ratings, which should bring down their overall appraisal rating. Simple, really! Except, of course, in reality it gives rise to difficult conversations and conflict. Ironically, it is also common for competency assessments to be used to inflate someone's overall rating where they failed to achieve target. The way through this is by having an appraisal process that is as streamlined as possible, and by having line managers skilled at holding open and meaningful conversations about pay and performance. When these are regular conversations, monthly or perhaps every six to eight weeks, there is less likely to be conflict at appraisal time. These are more likely to be regular conversations when vision, values and strategies are aligned, and when line managers' skills have been built over time, through consistent processes, concepts and messages. In other words, through talent management.

Bekaert's appraisal documentation is an example of a streamlined process. People are reviewed against five business targets and five critical skills, which are known at Bekaert as 'Ways of Working' (WOWs). There are five WOWs on the appraisal documentation, and for each there is space to specify any job-specific requirements, so these can be expanded or tailored to suit each role and each person. Bekaert's WOWs relate clearly to its competency profile, its values and its 'Better together' vision. Each WOW is discussed and there is an option to add two additional targets under WOWs, if this is necessary. All targets are weighted. People apportion weightings for each target, within an overall percentage for business targets and another for the WOWs.

Undoubtedly, however well embedded values are in an organization, there are managers paying lip service to appraisals, some people are cynical about values, and there are conflicts over appraisal ratings. What these organizations have reached, however, is the point where the critical mass use appraisals effectively and have made organizational values their own.

For those readers who feel their organizations are far away from an aligned approach, or from top-level support, or from a talent mindset, perhaps you can be heartened by the idea that once you achieve a critical uptake, this will create its own momentum and good practice will spread.

360-degree or multi-source feedback

360-degree feedback has become a powerful tool of performance management. It has also grown steadily in popularity partly because delivery through the internet has made systems easy to run and administer.

One reason for its growing use is that, with many organizations having more people than ever working in flexible, project, virtual or matrix teams, many line managers have wider spans of control and no direct or complete line of sight over the work of their staff. They therefore need more information to help them form an accurate picture of performance, which may come through inputs from project leaders or the other 'dotted line' reporting manager or from a 360-degree feedback exercise that forms part of the performance appraisal.

However, the use of 360-degree feedback has both pros and cons, whether it is included in performance appraisal or used solely for development planning.

The premise behind 360-degree feedback is that people have to work and achieve results together. Therefore insight into how your behaviour impacts on others should help you develop your performance and improve your results. Moreover, the people who work closely with an employee see that person's behaviour in settings and circumstances that a line manager may not, which gives a more rounded view of their performance.

However, a number of recent studies indicate that 360-degree feedback programmes may be failing to match their promise. Jai Ghorpade, a professor of management at San Diego State University, wrote in the Academy of Management Executive that, 'while it delivers valuable feedback, the 360-degree concept has serious problems relating to privacy, validity and effectiveness'.[1] Ghorpade reported that out of more than 600 feedback studies, one-third found improvements in performance, one-third reported decreases in performance and the rest reported no impact at all. John Sullivan, professor of human resource management at San Francisco State University, says, 'there is no data showing that [360-degree feedback] actually improves productivity, increases retention, decreases grievances or is superior to forced ranking and standard performance appraisal systems. It sounds good, but there is no proof it works.'[2]

These views match my own experiences where I find, increasingly, that people take from 360-degree feedback only what they want and file the rest. In these circumstances it becomes a ritual dance that wastes both time and money. The whole point of 360-degree feedback is to bring out issues that need to be addressed and provide an opportunity to address them. If you avoid difficult issues that arise because, well, they are difficult, then the exercise loses credibility and support; it becomes a bureaucratic form-filling exercise: a game and not a management tool. Consider the example of T, a larger-than-life senior manager with great business-getting skills. His 360-degree feedback showed that he was neither communicating with nor supporting his staff and there was an undertone of bullying; they respected his technical skills but clearly disliked working for him. This was a marvellous opportunity to work with T to improve his management skills or to reposition him so that he would do less damage. Unfortunately, everyone was scared of him and did nothing. His director did not even discuss the 360-degree feedback with him. So there was an escalation in turnover among his direct reports, who were disappointed and disillusioned by the outcome of the 360-degree feedback. Consultants Watson Wyatt say in their 2001 HCI report that they believe a poorly implemented 360-degree feedback can actually be detrimental to company performance.[3]

Although I have known 360-degree feedback produce disastrous results I have also experienced outstanding results, which makes it worth considering the causes of those failures and what makes for success.

Failure

Often failure results from substantial gaps between the organization's business objectives and what 360-degree feedback programmes measure. Competencies are so broad that they are not relevant to the average and they do not pick up on specific interpersonal and cultural problems in the organization at a specific time. Assuring context relevance is not easy and calls for a very different type of competency on the part of the HR professionals and others who are helping companies to use 360-degree feedback.

A study by Eichinger and Lombardo of the accuracy of those who are rating colleagues shows that the length of time that they have known the person being rated has the most significant effect on the accuracy of a 360-degree review.[4] The study shows that subjects in the group 'known for one to three years' are the most accurate, followed by 'known for less than one year', followed by 'known for three to five years', and the least accurate being 'known for more than five years'. It concludes that the most accurate ratings come from knowing the person long enough to get past first impressions, but not so long as to begin to generalize favourably. The implication is that misplaced loyalty can stand in the way of honest assessment. Moreover, multi-rater assessments regularly generate conflicting opinions. For example, how is an employee to react when his manager gives him negative ratings while feedback from his direct reports and peers is satisfactory? This can be a strength of 360-degree feedback, as it enables someone to reflect on why one group or one person views their behaviour more favourably; but it also results in confusion and people are likely to take away the feedback that suits them rather than gain any development benefit.

A study reported in *Personnel Psychology*[5] found that each rater group brings natural biases. For example, supervisor feedback tends to be based on bottom-line results (Are tasks completed on time and well?), technical competence and whether an employee's behaviour draws complaints from clients. By contrast, direct reports base their reviews on factors such as trustworthiness, willingness to involve them in decisions and the interest shown in their professional development. Peers who lack perspective on their colleagues' day-to-day performance tend to focus on leadership potential. Their remarks often reflect opinions or whether the participant has the 'right stuff' to motivate and create a compelling vision for others to follow. None of these perspectives is wrong and all are valuable insights in creating a 360-degree view of performance. However, it is important that the person being reviewed and their line manager understand how the filters used by different groups affect their ratings. Often people are sent their 360-degree feedback without the opportunity of an individualized debrief or coaching session to help them make sense of these different perceptions and turn them into insights to develop performance.

As Vinson suggests, there is no way to determine whose feedback is accurate.[6] This has implications for the use of 360-degree feedback and certainly suggests that it should not be used as a direct input into appraisal ratings or pay awards.

Another common failing of these programmes is a lack of follow-up after feedback, which means that in most circumstances the opportunity for it to be an aid to development is lost.

Success

This review of the failings of 360-degree feedback also points the way to make it successful.

The key to developing performance is to have a good awareness of your preferred style of working and of relating to others, as well as understanding how you impact on people and situations. When you have this awareness, you can then choose if and how to develop your performance, do things differently or do new things. Receiving input from others can be especially valuable at performance appraisal time, to help you reflect on your performance over the past year and ahead to the next.

Some years ago, I helped a US investment bank introduce 360-degree feedback for performance appraisal in its foreign exchange dealing team. The bank's previous attempt at introducing such a process had led to mistrust and backstabbing. This time we involved everyone in designing the process and conducted an extensive communication programme about the exercise, discussing what we wanted to achieve and how everyone would benefit. We achieved outstanding results, not only in terms of higher satisfaction levels from staff with the quality of their appraisals, and especially their conversations with their line managers, but also in making a positive impact on the culture. For example, one of the managers found he had assessed one of his staff far more harshly than her colleagues had done. As a result, he reconsidered his judgment and concluded that, as she was the only woman on his team, he may have been applying inappropriate criteria. It helped this individual examine his attitudes about what makes for effective behaviours in the dealing environment. Moreover, by involving people in the design of the process, we raised awareness about behaviours; we also trained people to make more balanced judgments about their colleagues and encouraged better teamwork. In this case, not only did we achieve the purpose of better quality appraisals, we also impacted positively on the culture of the organization and, in this way, encouraged a talent mindset on the part of both line managers and their staff.

Overall, a highly successful part of this programme, and an approach I have used to good effect on other occasions, has been where I, as the external consultant and 'postbag' for the anonymous reports, have spent time with line managers interpreting the feedback for their direct reports and coaching them in holding a feedback conversation. At one and the same time, this gave line managers increased skills, it ensured individuals received appropriate feedback and guidance, and it helped line managers build effective relationships with their people.

When you first introduce 360-degree appraisal the following pointers will lead to success. Eventually, it can become less formal and organized by the employees themselves (see Chapter 9, KPMG case study):

1 Be clear about your purpose. Clarifying purpose will help identify how to use the results. For example, is the purpose to help development or is it to provide input into the conversation between line manager and staff? Is it to provide a check on the line manager's performance assessments? Avoid using 360-degree feedback to compensate for line manager weakness in providing meaningful feedback. Avoid it being a direct input into pay.

2 Involve as many people as possible in the design of the process.

3 Communicate widely so that everyone is clear about its goals, what it will be used for and what is expected of them.

4 Train people to be able to give and receive feedback.

5 Ensure that the questionnaire is relevant. 360-degree feedback must be based on observable behaviours. If people are to be rated against a competency profile, make sure this encompasses or relates to the behavioural capabilities discussed in the previous chapter so that it is an integral part of your talent management system. Include free text options for people to respond to some open questions.

6 Moderate the process until it has become embedded. Even with well-designed processes in organizations with high trust levels, a thoughtless comment can be damaging. A moderator should go back to the originator of a questionable comment to explain and

clarify. The aim of 360-degree feedback is to motivate and support, not demotivate or damage.

7   Provide a debriefing or coaching session to help individuals make sense of their feedback and follow up on the results. This may be an external coach or a specially trained internal coach or line manager.

8   Provide confidentiality and anonymity. In some organizations people organize their own 360-degree feedback, as and when they wish, by e-mailing colleagues and inviting feedback, which may or may not be anonymous. I have known this work well, but only in a culture of trust and collaboration and where 360-degree feedback is well embedded.

9   Reinforce your cultural objectives in designing the process, communicating it and deciding how people will receive their results.

10 Check the process regularly if you have been running 360-degree feedback for some time: it may have declined and become an empty exercise.

11 Follow through. Put in place coaching or training, or line manager support, to help people develop action plans and follow these through.

12 Ask, 'How will a 360-degree programme help line managers?' The process should then be designed so that it will either help line managers have meaningful conversations or develop their own skills.

In summary, 360-degree appraisal depends upon commitment and a supportive atmosphere. 'Poor morale at the outset or poor implementation can lead to its use as a weapon. If an organization is in trauma, then the immediate causes must be dealt with before trying to use a sophisticated process that depends for its success upon commitment and mutual support. Subsequently, 360-degree appraisal can be used as part of the healing process and can exorcize the demons, leading to a more rapid turnaround. 360-degree feedback incorporated into performance appraisal is an asset in many circumstances. It is a check on decisions that are made about people, and a way of helping people reflect on their performance. It also provides a framework for line manager–employee discussions on performance and development.'[7]

Measuring the impact people at the top have on employee engagement

The top team are the people who make things happen. They impact directly on engagement. It follows therefore that we need to have a way of measuring this impact for each person. Some organizations use engagement survey scores as an input into the bonus payments of their top team.

One valuable initiative I have been involved in was to run a 360-degree feedback programme for the directors of an organization and then draw comparisons between their individual results and those from an employee engagement survey. It proved particularly useful to compare the person's 360-degree feedback results with the survey data for the whole organization and for the director's own area of operation. This helped the directors to understand how their behaviours impacted on their organization.

For this exercise I designed a questionnaire that linked directly to the organization's senior leadership profile and to a previous assessment exercise that we had run for all directors. The questionnaire generated a report, which I analysed for each person. First, I set out their 360-degree results in relation to the previous assessment exercise, bringing explanation and insight into the feedback that 360-degree on its own lacks. I similarly analysed the employee engagement survey results, for the organization as a whole and for the individual's own area. Finally I incorporated all findings and correlations in a report, which I then explained to each person in a confidential coaching session. It was striking for many directors to see the close correlations between their personal feedback and employee engagement results. For example, the comments made about one director in areas concerning communication and feedback corresponded directly to employee engagement scores on similar criteria.

While I did not recommend that the directors shared their 360-degree feedback results, I drew up a 'team report', which showed common areas of concern and gave ideas to address these. I also pointed out who could be able to lead in raising engagement levels for a particular set of indicators. For example, in the communication category one director, who received high ratings in his 360-degree feedback, was the obvious choice to lead on this.

One benefit of this exercise was to show to the business's leaders just how much of a direct impact their behaviour had on the business. People at the top are aware of the impact they have by virtue of their technical contribution and their decisions, but do not always appreciate the impact of how they behave and what they say. This initiative also showed the value of integrating processes. In this case, the link between these two activities led to the top team putting more effort into following through on both than they had done on previous such exercises.

Reward

One of the aims of talent management is to differentiate between levels of performance but in a way that recognizes that everyone is important. The company's reward policy needs to support this, whether through the way it gives extrinsic, monetary rewards or intrinsically through a recognition programme.

Does pay motivate? This question has been extensively researched and debated. One answer that always emerges is that pay levels that are perceived to be unfair are hugely demotivating. This reaction seems to be deeply rooted in our animal nature: recent research showed that dogs, perceiving that others were rewarded more for performing the same tricks would 'sulk' and become uncooperative. Guest and Conway have shown that perceived fairness, alongside trust, is at the core of a positive, engaging and high-performance-generating psychological contract in the workplace.[8] Truss *et al* find dissatisfaction with pay to be a primary factor limiting the engagement levels of UK employees, with less than a third of them trusting their organization's senior management.[9] Reilly and Brown similarly claim that huge salary differentials weaken loyalty and erode the internal talent pool.[10] It is clear that perceived fairness of reward is essential to create the talent mindset that we are aiming for as well as for our entire approach to talent management.

To say that money does or does not actively motivate is rather too simplistic. One of the conclusions we can draw from the various studies is that the motivational mix varies for each person and is also likely to change over the course of their life and career. The lesson is that pay can be an effective motivator, but line managers still need to work on additional motivators such as providing challenging and stretching work opportunities.

Non-financial recognition is an important part of the reward mix. This ranges from sending thank you e-mails to running formal prize-winning schemes. From my experience, the most effective form of non-financial reward is where someone's contribution is widely recognized. This recognition must come from the person's line manager, but from other directions also, such as senior management, or perhaps some form of public acknowledgement. For example, with one organization we trained an internal cadre of coaches. They received no extra money for this but absorbed it into their workload. Those whose line managers recognized their effort and contribution were significantly more motivated than those whose line managers paid it scant attention.

I referred earlier to the importance of differentiating levels of performance. High performers especially benefit from recognition on a wider platform. Consistency is important, however. I worked recently in an organization where the top team was constantly battling over whose business goals were the more important. The knock-on effect was that some high performance went unrecognized, while lesser contributions were publicly lauded. Needless to say, this caused considerable discontent.

The concept of financial rewards linked to performance arouses strong feelings among supporters and opponents. The most powerful argument advanced for contingent financial rewards is that it is only fair to recognize achievement with a share of what the individual has created – blurring the line between employee and owner. Many also see pay-for-performance schemes as preferable to the alternatives of service-related pay progression or spot rates. Performance pay may well be a key objective and there is a lot of evidence that many employees agree that it is fair for those who contribute more to be paid more.

John Stacey Adams's pay equity theory is helpful here. According to this, we arrive at our measure of fairness – equity – by comparing our balance of effort and reward, and other factors such as the perceived ratio of input to output, with that enjoyed by other people, whom we deem to be relevant reference points ('referent' others).[11] Crucially this means that equity does not depend on our input-to-output ratio alone – it depends on our comparison with others who comprise the marketplace as we see it. This helps to explain why people are so strongly affected by the situations (and views and gossip) of colleagues, friends, etc in establishing their own personal sense of fairness or equity in their own work situations.

The implications of this for talent management are considerable. Pay for performance fits with one of our prime talent management notions, which is the importance of knowing who your high performers are and of giving them appropriate and balanced recognition. It can provide the incentive to differentiate performance levels. However, in our case for talent, we also emphasize that everyone matters, and Adams's pay equity theory reminds us that it is important to ensure that both recipient and colleagues perceive a differentiated pay award as fair.

The basis on which a contingent pay award is made needs to be clear, not only in the policy but in the way it is communicated by line managers and supported by cultural values. This means being clear about the difference between a steady contributor and a high performer and ensuring that both feel differentials are fair and that both their contributions are recognized.

Adams's pay equity theory refers not only to how we perceive internal relativities but also to differences between individuals' remuneration packages and what they feel they could attain in the marketplace. If an organization's pay structure is far off the market position or if individuals with similar skills are being paid widely different salaries for undertaking the same job content, then there is a problem, especially in cases where variances are exacerbated on the basis of gender, race or ethnicity. This part of the pay equity theory underlines the importance of open and clear communication of the basis on which pay awards are made. Communication should include market and job comparisons so that people can clearly see how they relate to others in the marketplace.

The practical difficulties with contingent pay have tended to revolve around the perceived and actual unfairness of the performance appraisal and management processes that act as the basis for the determination of pay awards. Many employers need to devote more attention to this, if the performance-related rewards they make are to be generally accepted and perceived to be fair and therefore motivating. Fair pay and truly performance-related pay are complementary, not competing, reward goals. They both depend on accurate, consistent and fair assessment of performance or contribution, a clearly articulated basis on which pay differences and overall pay policies are determined. A climate of trust in the organization is also important.

In summary, the following points are critical from a talent management viewpoint and it is recommended that talent management and reward specialists work closely together here.

1 *Reward strategy.* The written reward strategy must encourage the behaviours and competencies that are aimed for in the talent strategy. It should assert the importance of fair, non-discriminatory pay in the organization. It should define what fairness means for your organization: for example, how under-performers are treated, the stance towards equal pay and how the external market is taken into account for recruitment and retention.

2 *Communication.* Having fairness enshrined as a key reward principle in your organization's employee handbook is not worth the paper it is written on unless employees perceive the principle to be evident in practice. This requires a two-pronged approach: one is through corporate communication and the other is through the involvement of line managers.

The basis for pay differences needs to be clearly defined and communicated as part of your reward principles. Moreover, it is recommended that you regularly ask staff what they think about their rewards. Leading organizations openly provide information to all employees when pay awards are determined. This includes showing market comparisons, identifying roles where salaries have drifted away from appropriate internal or external relativities and explaining clearly the basis on which across-the-board increases have been determined as well as the basis on which individual increases have been awarded. This information is given to all employees, and communication packs are also prepared for line managers to support them in having meaningful conversations with their staff about pay.

3 *Line managers.* As the Black Box research demonstrates, first-line managers are the critical linkage between reward principles and intentions on the one hand and the practical delivery and creation of a truly rewarding environment, conducive to high employee performance on the other.[12] Yet too often in the face of organizational restructuring, line managers have been left to cope with widening spans of control, increasingly complex and demanding pay and reward systems and a lack of local HR department support.

In my experience, many organizations fail to involve line managers in determining pay awards; and few line managers hold meaningful conversations with their employees about their pay award. This goes counter to our talent management approach, which emphasizes the importance of such discussions between line manager and employee. Pay is a major part of an individual's relationship with the organization. Leading organizations allocate a pool of funds to line managers who are then held accountable for distributing this. They are also required to justify their decisions. This often includes meeting other line managers in the unit to discuss pay awards together so as to achieve consistency and cross-department comparisons. Senior managers are then required to review and discuss these proposals and justifications. This process helps identify problems, such as inconsistencies, favouritism or discrimination. The pay decision is then openly discussed between line manager and individual. It is hard to claim that line managers are critical to driving high levels of employee engagement if they are excluded from any role in pay discussions. Moreover, line managers cannot truly take on a talent mindset if they do not fully appreciate how pay decisions affect different people and how they affect the motivational mix.

Training line managers in your reward policy and in holding open and direct conversations about reward is advised. HR business partners should work closely with line managers so that they understand the basis on which pay has been awarded and to support them in holding conversations about this with their staff. The line manager's line manager also has a role here in supporting line managers in what can be a difficult conversation.

Performance appraisal conclusions

I would now like to bring this discussion back to the performance appraisal system.

'Can't live with it, can't live without it.' This sums up how most people feel about performance appraisal. On the one hand, employees and line managers alike usually find the annual performance appraisal a valuable opportunity to take stock of what happened over the previous year and plan for the next. It's like going up in a helicopter and getting a whole perspective of the past year and the year ahead. This helicopter view generates a different kind of discussion from the regular ones about a single piece of work. In particular, it leads to better planning of the year ahead, especially when connected to the business planning cycle. The downside of performance appraisal is that it takes up a great deal of management time. This is especially the case in businesses such as professional service firms, whose flat hierarchy gives line managers large numbers of people to appraise. Many have found a way around this by establishing people management leaders who handle such processes. However, as illustrated in the case study example in Chapter 3, this works better where being a people management leader is recognized as a career-enhancing role. This gives more credence to performance appraisal and makes people feel it is worthwhile.

Matrix structures and flexible teams add to the complication: increasingly line managers do not have a direct line of sight over the work of the people they are expected to appraise. Collecting information from different parties and making sense of it can be problematic.

Especially keeping in mind some of the points about appraisal ratings and pay awards, what is required to make this process as effective as it can be? Consider the following:

1 Online solutions have made the collection and storage of data easier. Documents and procedures are often too complicated and bureaucratic but putting them online offers the opportunity to simplify.

2 Self-appraisal can lighten the line manager's role. From my experience, too many firms require both line managers and individuals to complete documents, then compare and discuss them. My preference is for the individual to complete the documentation and for the line manager to discuss only the important points or differences of perception. The conversation is then straightforward and less time-consuming. Where 360-degree feedback is incorporated into the appraisal process, this should be used, together with self-appraisal, so that it facilitates the conversation and inputs into development planning.

3 Performance appraisal often covers too many aims. Narrowing these and streamlining them into different processes is helpful. The best split is to base performance appraisal around objectives and performance ratings and to have a separate development review that covers development, potential and aspiration and leads to the 'three-stage' development plan discussed in the next chapter. Capability profiling or development centre feedback reports, also covered in the next chapter, can be integrated into this development review with the benefit of facilitating the conversation.

LEARNING POINTS

- Performance appraisal and reward policies send out strong cultural messages to people about organizational priorities. These messages must be consistent with your talent management strategy.

- It is important to differentiate levels of performance so that high performers are recognized as such. Pay-for-performance schemes are beneficial but must be perceived as fair and consistent, and, as with criteria for promotion, must transmit appropriate messages about what makes for success.

- Performance appraisals need to be streamlined. Creating one system for performance review that links to pay and a separate one that focuses on development and career works better than most current systems, which try to achieve too much. Including competencies and values in performance reviews reinforces their importance. Line managers should be given accountability for being effective talent managers by making this part of their performance review.

- Line managers should be trained and supported in discussing pay with their employees.

- 360-degree feedback must be implemented so that it leads to real development. It is valuable to link 360-degree feedback for the top team to the organization's employee survey to give members of the top team a better understanding of how their behaviour impacts on the performance of the organization.

References

1 Ghorpade, J (2000) Managing six paradoxes of 360-degree feedback, *Academy of Management Executive*, vol 14, pp 140–50

2 Sullivan, J (1998) HR program evaluation template: 360-degree feedback. Retrieved from http://www.drjohnsullivan.com/articles/1998/net12.htm on 2 February 2004

3 Watson Wyatt Human Capital Index®(2002) *Human capital as a lead indicator of shareholder value*, February

4 Eichinger, R W and Lombardo, M M (2004) Patterns of rater accuracy in 360-degree feedback, *Human Resource Planning*, vol 27

5 Mount, M K, Judge, J A, Scullen, S E, Sytsma, M R and Hezlett, S A (1998) Trait, rater and level effects in 360-degree performance, *Personnel Psychology*, **51** (3)

6 Vinson, M (1996) The pros and cons of 360-degree feedback: Making it work, *Training and Development*, April

7 Caplan, J (2000) 360-degree feedback for performance appraisal, *Training and Management Development Methods*, vol 14, No. 3, MCB University Press, Australia

8 Guest, D and Conway, N (2004) *Employee Well-being and the Psychological Contract*, CIPD, London

9 Truss, C *et al* (2006) *Working life: Employee attitudes and engagement*, CIPD, London

10 Reilly, P and Brown, D (2008) Employee engagement: what is the relationship with reward management?, *World at Work*, 4th quarter

11 http://www.businessballs.com/adamsequitytheory.htm

12 Purcell, J *et al* (2003) *Understanding the People and Performance Link: Unlocking the Black Box*, CIPD, London

Development

07

FIGURE 7.1 Development

Most people want a career or a developing future. The Black Box and other studies considered in Chapter 2 provide evidence that career, training and development are key factors that lead to improved employee engagement and, therefore, improved business performance. The Black Box study reveals that 'employees have expectations ... beyond just doing the job'.[1] It suggests that HR policies on careers and training are the most important in influencing employee attitudes and helping to create positive discretionary behaviour.

This gets to the heart of talent management, but, of course, it is also part of the learning and development agenda, and of organization development (OD). While it is the ideas that are important, not their labels, it does help understanding to clarify the difference between these disciplines and my use of the terms. 'Learning and development' are an important part of talent management but they tend to focus on helping people develop performance in their current role. They therefore deliver much but not all of the talent management strategy, which is more future focused and emphasizes developing people for organizational change and along their identified, longer-term career path. The term 'organizational development' is widely used in at least two distinct ways but, however you view it, OD overlaps considerably with my view of talent management and, throughout this book, is included within it. When I use the term organizational development, I do so in the sense of moving the organization towards its future goals, not in the sense of a discipline within HR.

In this chapter, I continue to explore the potential of an integrated talent management system. I look first at methods to assess development needs, and then consider development solutions that reinforce my talent management approach. Space does not permit me to cover in depth all the areas of development, learning, training, coaching, etc. I also consider concepts and initiatives that will help you create a talent mindset and make development effective.

Integrated talent management

Being able to identify someone to fill a role quickly or take on a completely new challenge or move into untried waters is a major aim of talent management. Growing your own talent to combat skills shortages or to enable you to become an employer of choice are also key, as is the need to support people in taking on the capabilities that will enable the organization to adapt to change as it happens.

These are not short-term aims that can be satisfied through one-off initiatives or ad hoc learning and development programmes. These are business needs requiring a consistent, cohesive approach to help people build their skills and understanding over time. In other words, they require an integrated talent management system.

In Chapter 5, I showed how you can extract behavioural capabilities from your mix of competencies; and that you can use these as the cornerstone of an integrated talent management system. You do that by referring all your HR activities and processes to these capabilities. For example, I described their use as selection criteria for job appointments but also to broaden discussion during performance appraisals.

Starting your development journey

I believe passionately that the more complete the insight into your performance, the more likely that you will understand your strengths and preferences and how to leverage these, and, similarly, your weaknesses and how to compensate for them. Self-awareness is the bedrock of personal development because it permits a comparison of current with desired capabilities and therefore points the way to what needs to be done to achieve those goals. It is how people can become the best they can be.

Raising your self-awareness involves some kind of assessment. This is different from assessment to make selection or pay decisions, or for assigning appraisal ratings. Even though in these cases the data generated should also inform a development plan, they nonetheless serve primarily to establish a cut-off point: you match the criteria or you don't at this point in time. The prime purpose of the assessment we use here, on the other hand, sets the start of your development journey. It may use some of the same methods and techniques but its different purpose means it should be positioned differently and the data generated must be applied differently.

There are two principal methods of assessment for starting this development journey. These are the new online profiling tools that have emerged in recent years, and development centres, which are a more traditional tool.

Online profiling

There are several online tools now available. Where these can be linked to your behavioural capabilities they are effective mechanisms for making an integrated talent management system happen. I do not wish to promote any one product, not least because it is not the product that is important but the way it is used and positioned to create an integrated system offering flexibility and value for money. However, it is impossible to describe an integrated system and its benefits without referring to a particular tool. I am, therefore, basing this discussion around one I know well, Iperquest®.

Iperquest is a proprietary model of behavioural effectiveness. It comprises behavioural capabilities that fall mostly within the natural and adapting clusters on Roberts's framework[2]. The capabilities contained within this model relate to the mental processes and behaviours that underpin successful performance: how you think, relate to others, do things, manage your emotions and handle change. Because they are fundamental qualities they can be related to how they affect an individual at work but avoid the problem competencies typically have, of not keeping up with change: competencies being defined in relation to that work rather than delving beneath to underlying behaviours. Clearly these capabilities also offer causal links between behaviours and performance effectiveness, helping you understand how behaving in a certain way affects the results you achieve at work.

There are many different ways of positioning these capabilities to match business and talent management goals. It is helpful to return to ABC Engineering to help our consideration of these different ways.

ABC had a competency framework that had been used for recruitment but little else. It was also poorly understood and inconsistently interpreted. The head of learning and development was keen to have a framework that could serve various different purposes and that the company could use to integrate some of its people processes. We therefore decided to replace this framework entirely with one based on the Iperquest capabilities that best matched the organization's future challenges.

Together with the capability framework, we launched a profiling tool, which is an online questionnaire that accompanies the Iperquest behavioural model. It gave people the opportunity to benchmark themselves against the 'capability set' for their grade. They received a profile that identified strengths and development areas; so this tool was both self-diagnostic and an action planner. It also contained guidance to help users discuss their profiles with their line manager.

Let's take Gabriella as an example. One aspect of her profile reveals that she takes a detailed approach to drawing up plans and shows she prefers to gain a thorough understanding before taking a decision. Relating this feedback to her performance, Gabriella realizes this explains why she is slow to adapt to change, but it also explains why she takes the responsibility of checking thoroughly to ensure that change is well implemented. She can use the profile as a guide for self-study or as part of a coaching process to develop her behaviour, and can draw on supporting materials on the company's intranet for these purposes. The profile also facilitates Gabriella's conversation with her line manager, who can use it to give feedback on her performance, discuss development and identify work opportunities that will enable her to deploy her strengths. By focusing on her strengths, Gabriella's profile has given her more confidence to take on bigger challenges, but also indicates how she might develop her behaviour to tackle them. She can check on the company's intranet to see which capabilities are required for different roles in the organization and plan her development accordingly.

At ABC Engineering, we trained a pool of volunteers from across the business as feedback coaches to help individuals understand their profile and how to take it forward. This part of the programme not only gave individuals useful personal skills but we were also able to encourage cross-functional working that had an impact on the spirit of collaboration – which was very important as the organization operated under a matrix structure. The coaches became ambassadors for the processes we introduced and were instrumental in championing and embedding what we had done. The support of the top team also had an enormous impact here, making the exercise real. In many companies, such programmes might be introduced with a memo encouraging line managers to be coaches and encouraging colleagues to support one another but then – nothing; and when senior executives hold performance reviews with their staff they never mention these things, just focus on the technical. In this case, through getting active involvement at a senior level, we got them to ask important questions such as, 'How are you getting on as a feedback coach?' and 'What is it doing for you?'

Receiving Iperquest profiles raised self-awareness and was the start of the development journey for people. The organization also introduced a range of training and development programmes that related to the capabilities. These included an online campus with materials for either self-study or peer coaching. Note that the behavioural capability framework and profiling process aligned individual strengths and development to identified business success criteria. People were now aware of the importance of behavioural capabilities and especially which ones would be important to the organization. They became more client oriented and open to new ideas. The next phase of business development also demanded an ability to work with outsource partners, so many people had to develop influencing skills and the ability to suggest and advise when they had no formal authority to direct or impose decisions. Step one in this process made people aware of what was expected. It raised their self-awareness and also interest.

This approach may not sound very different from what is common practice in most organizations but it has several distinguishing features. One is the opportunity it gives you to focus people on the behaviours that are valued by the organization. This increases the likelihood of people understanding and paying attention to them, and consequently they are more likely to use them to develop their skills. The second distinguishing feature is the level of analysis and insight offered by the system illustrated here, and those like it, to help people leverage their strengths and plan development. Third, the practical simplicity of an online tool enables you to include large numbers of people relatively easily and cheaply.

When you implement such a tool, it is important to be clear about its purposes. At ABC we positioned the tool to build a coaching capability in the organization, as well as to spearhead continuous learning and development, and emphasize the firm's cultural aim of driving better peer support and collaboration. In other instances, I have focused on training line managers to use the process to develop their coaching style of management, or used it for team development where it helps people recognize what each brings to the table and how to benefit from each other's strengths and preferences.

Development centres

Development centres grew out of assessment centres and, as the names imply, have contrasting purposes. Assessment centres are designed to assess suitability for jobs, whereas a development centre helps people develop skills and behaviours that are desired by their employer. They encourage continuous development and learning, as a result of which people are generally better able to adapt swiftly to a new and demanding opportunity. In this way, they facilitate rapid career advancement or career changes and are especially beneficial for meeting 'new world' needs.

The link between development centres and organizational culture is powerful. In 2005 Scala, together with our ACE partners, surveyed the use of development centres in 93 UK organizations, employing between 1,000 and 93,000 employees, and compared these findings with case study organizations from across Europe. Among the latter, merger and acquisition, culture change or reorganization were the key drivers of development centre programmes. Others were the need to replace a 'silo' structure and mentality with a more cohesive and global approach to career and personal development. In some cases, large investments were made in development centres to support the business strategy or brand development. Several businesses used the programme to convey a top-down message that encouraged everyone to invest in being a good people manager so that this would be part of the DNA of the organization. Another organization used the centres to convey that all employees had a right to receive specific, positive and constructive feedback, which they believed was the key to unleashing talent. This enabled them to embed the mindset that everyone has a right to know what their line manager and the organization think of their performance.

The following were cited by respondents to this survey as the main benefits of development centre programmes:

- awareness to individual of ability and potential;
- enables organization to identify high-potential employees;
- less subjective approach to identifying skills and development gaps;
- enables staff to see a career path;
- excellent retention tool;
- identifying development needs and meeting those needs in all individuals;
- motivation of staff, leading to increase in company performance;
- helps continue growth of company.

Typical comments from our survey about how participants viewed development centres were: 'People say how marvellous it is that the organization is doing this for me,' 'People see the development centre as a unique opportunity to understand themselves better, to look in the mirror, and get immersed in themselves with the support of professionals.'

As with the profiling process, if you implement development centres, it is vital to be clear about their purpose and who may participate. A development centre programme that communicates particular corporate values, helps people plan their development in line with organizational capabilities, and gives the organization a better understanding of the people it employs is wholly consistent with an inclusive approach to talent management, with its emphasis on valuing individuals. It will naturally take care of high-potential people but will also help others refresh and refocus their skills or develop their careers. It can also enable better performance development planning for weaker or marginal performers.

Development centres risk the perception that they are a means of weeding out poor performers, and so how you communicate about them to avoid this is vital. Practically, however, you can't include everyone and so participants must be selected on clear business needs and not because people feel they lose status if they are not chosen. The most common criteria are to run the centres for line managers at a certain level, perhaps to raise people management skills as in the examples above, or for those new to a management role. In all cases the criteria and objectives must be clearly communicated to everyone.

For many organizations, giving a sense of corporate identity and values while enabling people to maintain their cultural and personal individuality presents a real challenge. Capabilities (or competencies) meet this challenge by creating consistency, while also allowing scope for local adaptation. Through consistent use, you build pictures in people's minds about 'how we do things around here' and what is important to organizational success. Capabilities also enable you to open career paths internationally or across divisions by providing common criteria to describe roles and assess suitability. In this way, you achieve a balance between consistency and quality on the one hand and local adaptation and autonomy on the other.

Some years ago, for example, I worked on a global programme with Diesel, the clothing brand. To quote Diesel's group HR director, 'This is not about identifying high flyers, but it is about helping the management team and the company to grow as a team.'[3] She added, 'It is also about giving managers a sense of Diesel's corporate identity and values, the "Diesel planet" ... yet without losing cultural and personal individuality.'

From our experience at ACE, development centres are most effective when they:

1 Provide a clear and energized starting-point to the development process. A well-conducted centre is the best way of getting people to buy into and take responsibility for their own development plans. Future planning will be based around behaviour that took place during the exercises, and the priorities for development will be apparent.

2 Give people the opportunity to take part in simulations of the job, or competencies, upon which their development is focused, and receive high-quality feedback to plan development.

3 Enable people to assess their own performance and diagnose their strengths and limitations. This can be achieved in diverse ways, such as using self-report questionnaires or exercises that encourage reflection. My ACE colleagues at Interselect in the Netherlands have developed an innovative way of videoing people during practical exercises and using these videos to encourage people to self-assess and explore development opportunities with a trained facilitator. This combines an effective and well-used training room tool with development centre methods.

4 Enable people to identify their career aspirations and gain insights about themselves, such as becoming more aware of their learning style and career preferences. Development centres facilitate a joint approach in which the organization and participants collaborate to make career and development plans. This is generally highly motivating for people.

5 Involve line managers. One best-practice case study in the Scala/ACE research showed that involving line managers in the feedback session with their staff encouraged them to support their employees' development more actively than they had done previously.[4] Involving line managers as observers and assessors is also recommended. This gives them ownership of the process and they bring a business relevance to it. It also provides them with highly effective training. Whereas traditional leadership development or coaching skills training at some point leaves you to get on with it, being an observer gives you both the training and the practice. The skills involved are important for a coaching style of management: giving feedback, supporting development and reviewing performance.

6 Are evaluated and validated so that you can track that they continue to produce reliable data and are in step with changing needs.

Profiling processes and development centres do, of course, have pitfalls. These are the most common to watch out for:

- Be transparent when communicating the process and its purpose. Complete transparency over the use of assessment data is essential to building trust. Communicate clearly upfront what data will be generated, who will see feedback reports and be party to the data, and explain how the data will be used. Commonly, a programme is introduced to help personal development and data remain with the individual. Later, however, needs may change. For example, it may be realized that the data could inform succession planning – but using it for a different purpose than was originally promised can destroy trust. Allow for this upfront. Consider all possible uses of the data and reserve the right to use them in these ways in the future. Remember, however, that assessment results must be treated as tentative and less reliable as time passes after the event.

- Avoid over-engineering by aiming to cover too many capabilities. Much can be achieved by focusing on the behavioural capability dimensions required for success in the future, such as adaptability and learning.

- It is absolutely vital to have follow-up development programmes in place at the outset. Especially when these methods are rolled out to everyone, or to a large group, it is important to keep pace with the demands and enthusiasm they generate. Development centres, especially, raise expectations and the challenge then becomes how to make sure people are getting what they want and not losing motivation and momentum.

- Make sure the capabilities used at development centres link to those used at assessment centres. Build bridges with recruiters to ensure consistency of both capabilities and message.

Processes such as capability profiling and development centres offer developmental and motivational benefits to individuals, which directly link to the factors around careers and development that enhance employee engagement. They are powerful ways to drive organizational culture, focus people on behaviour and encourage continuous learning. This creates flexibility and adaptability to change. Both processes produce profile reports and when line managers are trained to use them, these facilitate those all-important conversations about careers and development. They also enable the organization to gain a better understanding of its workforce, which is essential if you are to react swiftly to change.

To return to our consideration of an integrated talent management system, the point is that it consists of a range of processes and tools that offer something to everyone. It does this in a way that creates shared values and understanding.

While profiling and development centres bring considerable advantages, and their flexibility of use offers value for money, they are unlikely to suit everyone or every purpose, and it may not be possible for you to offer them widely, or maybe at all. In any event, put additional and alternative options in place. Here are some possibilities:

- 360-degree feedback is less versatile than the options discussed here, but is nonetheless useful.

- The use of wikis (see Chapter 1: websites that allow anyone to create or edit pages), social networking, e-learning and so on offer valuable ways of encouraging learning, sharing information and connecting people globally and across organizational boundaries. Take advantage of these new technologies to disseminate capabilities, values and culture. The possibilities are endless and will change the nature of learning.

- New technologies also make it easy for people to learn about jobs and roles and therefore identify future career opportunities. They also make it easy for the organization to collect data about its people by asking them to complete internal CVs and so on.

Know your workforce

Especially within a successful organization, it's quite easy to identify people who are high performers, but identifying those who have the potential to move into something else is much harder. In a jobs market where employers often struggle to fill skilled vacancies, businesses simply cannot afford to lose people who may have hidden or underused talents simply because they have let them drift or become disenchanted. The development centre and profiling processes discussed here help you understand the skills, strengths and abilities of the people you employ, as well as their potential to take on new skills and new roles. This is particularly important when many organizations are changing their structures to meet the challenges of the business climate. This understanding enables you to identify someone to fill a role quickly, know whether they can take on a completely new challenge or move into untried waters, and understand the support they will require to do this. It is also, of course, a prime way of growing your own talent.

Achieving this level of flexibility in the workforce requires more than taking a note of who has which skills. It requires a mindset that values people for their strengths and preferences, seeks to understand their aspirations and is prepared to take a risk with someone and offer them an accelerated career path or an opportunity they may not have the exact experience for. Let's examine these concepts further.

Valuing people for their strengths and preferences

My approach to talent management is practical and pragmatic, developed from experience as well as research and analysis. It does, however, have a strong connection with the field of positive psychology, which is about 'optimal human functioning' – studying and understanding people at their best – and is the core concept on which this approach to talent management is based; and which should underpin an organization's talent management strategy and practices. It is also an important part of a talent mindset, which requires focusing on individuals' strengths and building their role around these. I recently met a professor from one of America's leading medical schools who reminded me how, years ago, when he was a manager at a British medical school, he had sought my advice on how to deal with a member of his lab team who was not able to perform the role as required. Dismissing this person or moving him into a different role were not available options. My advice was to change the requirements of the role. Everyone has strengths and preferences. Find out what this person does best and adapt the role to suit. This now high-ranking professor said he has managed on this basis since and it has served him exceptionally well.

In making talent important for everyone, a focus on strengths and preferences benefits individual development but also encourages a creative, positive working environment and good teamwork. It is important, nonetheless, for people to understand what they do less well and in what circumstances. This might help someone learn how to develop their behaviour to achieve better results or to venture beyond their comfort zone, or to help them understand how to compensate for a weakness by drawing on someone else's support. These are all important aspects of development.

This is an important message to emphasize consistently through your practices and processes and how you implement them.

It does not mean, however, that poor or even marginal performance should be ignored. Failure to address poor performance is a common problem. Often it occurs because managers fail to recognize poor performance early enough and it then becomes harder to address. A better understanding of capabilities generally leads to a better understanding of standards of performance, which in turn makes managers better at recognizing poor performance and more likely to deal with it.

Taking a risk

In Chapter 5, I discussed this topic in relation to recruitment but it is equally relevant in the context of development. Especially as organizations have fewer opportunities for career promotion, emphasis has been placed on advancing through sideways rather than upwards moves. This has tended to encourage attitudes to career progression that see people taking small career steps. The companies that are prepared to offer rapid advancement have generally been those undergoing rapid growth. However, fast-paced structural change is rendering such a risk-averse approach unworkable.

Talent management requires giving people stretching opportunities that take them beyond their comfort zone and possibly also take them into areas where they may need to acquire new skills and knowledge rapidly. This might seem to run counter to my suggestion of an approach that focuses on getting people to do what they do best, which could be seen as a risk-averse strategy. In fact, it reinforces the importance of understanding individual capabilities. People deliver their best performance when they are able to do what they do best every day. This is an important finding of Gallup's research into employee engagement.[5] It is not just about someone performing tasks or job roles they do best, but doing new things that use their best capabilities. Even so, knowing what causes performance shortfalls and being able to compensate for or overcome them is an important part of personal growth and development. Even more importantly, giving people a raised self-awareness that enables them to go beyond their comfort zones is absolutely crucial to development, especially for leadership roles, or to roles that require a big leap forward.

Building knowledge of behavioural capabilities gives the individual and the organization greater insight and understanding of what someone does best, and the capabilities to leverage when planning job opportunities. It helps take managers, especially, beyond the traditional thinking that to perform a role, someone must have done it before or at least something very similar.

Understanding aspirations and planning development

The CIPD 2009 survey into recruitment, retention and turnover revealed that 'promotion outside the organization (50 per cent) and changing career (49 per cent) remain the most common causes of voluntary turnover'.[6] This finding adds weight to the importance of understanding people's aspirations and matching these with opportunity.

A successful approach to use here is to encourage people to draw up a long-term development plan that sets out their aspirations over three career stages relating to three time spans and matches these with development opportunity:

- Stage 1 will be the immediate future. This is the period generally covered in performance appraisals. It should focus on what stretch and challenge are available in the current role, unless, of course, the person is new to the role and is still on a learning curve.

- Stage 2 will focus on medium-term development and the next possible role for the person, say within the next three to five years, and will aim to produce the capabilities they will need.

- Stage 3 will address longer-term ambitions, perhaps within the next six to ten years.

Roles in this case may not equate to actual positions but to present and future capabilities. The reports generated by profiling tools or development centres can be reference points around which line managers can structure conversations with their employees and help them draw up a development plan. When you do this it is surprisingly easy. In most cases people aim for something that they can start working towards now and it is probably what the organization needs too. This is especially the case if you have recruitment and goal setting right. So, for example, let's say that a project worker at head office aspires to being a project manager next and then wants to be out on site. The short-term aim to take a project manager role requires some influencing skills, while a posting on site requires development of technical knowledge plus a lot more skill in influencing. Both roles require this person to have more exposure to contractors. Let's say also that the line manager has identified that this person needs more confidence in dealing with outside teams and needs to build better relationships with them in order to do their current job better; so their line manager could open up opportunities for additional experience, perhaps supported by some studying or maybe a training course to help them build confidence at influencing.

The point is that it is often possible to open opportunities to people that will meet a short-term organizational need while also moving them towards longer-term career aspirations. If no current project exists, then, having identified a business and individual need that are aligned, you may start planning one. Importantly, this three-stage process takes care of ambitious high-potential people.

This longer-term perspective on development planning is flexible and can adapt to individual and business needs. If the business need or the individual's ambition changes, then there is little downside to either the individual or the business in pursuing such development. The costs are seldom significant as much of the development is delivered through experiences that are provided – and skills are never wasted. The business gains from the person's contribution and probably enhanced level of engagement. It lets people know they are valued and gives an indication of what the future might hold, without making commitments that can't be kept. It also adjusts better to people's changing expectations, such as in the professional services firm referred to in Chapter 4 that found employees becoming increasingly demanding, especially about career development and promotion prospects. This increasingly typical situation places considerable onus on businesses to provide development opportunity as well as identify potential.

Considering longer-term career aspirations also raises the question of what to do about people who are content to remain in the same job or who do not know what they want to do in the future. Development plans do not have to be about a new or different job but can equally be about what may become different in the current job or what could be done differently. Few jobs remain the same these days. It is probably helpful to encourage the person who does not know what might interest them next to network more across the organization. This may help them to identify areas of interest but, in any case, is likely to benefit them and their department by broadening their understanding of the organization and their personal links to others within it.

The importance of understanding aspirations and matching these with opportunity is another valuable message you must emphasize consistently through your talent management system.

Development solutions

I would like to turn now to learning and development methods and initiatives and will focus on discussing the importance of development through experience, which is a core concept of talent management and will touch on training and coaching. I then set out some case studies that offer outstanding examples of approaches to training, coaching and the use of collaborative learning through social networking.

Meaningful opportunity

The three-stage way of aligning organization and individual development depends on people believing that most learning and development come from actual work experience. Countless studies show that most of what people know and retain is from what they learn on the job through experience. Learning is something that happens continually. Talent management encourages this and creates an environment where experience is passed on and shared and where people coach each other naturally as part of their everyday routine.

Development by experience hinges on line managers' willingness and ability to provide opportunities to people to enable them to grow and develop in a way that meets their aspirations as well as business needs. This is a crucial line manager responsibility. I use the term 'meaningful opportunity' as a convenient, shorthand way of putting across the concept. It is also a useful term for an intranet portal or for e-learning materials to help people put the concept into practice.

Being willing and able to provide meaningful opportunity is a crucial line management responsibility. It requires understanding capabilities, insight into strengths and preferences and an awareness of aspirations. It also requires willingness to support someone by giving them regular feedback and encouraging them to reflect on their learning. A coach or colleague can perform these last responsibilities but making the opportunity available and giving recognition for achievement are clearly the role of the line manager.

Bekaert and Standard Chartered Bank are two organizations that have succeeded in embedding this approach, with the result that line managers are now open to the notion of identifying opportunities that can be opened to people within their existing job.

FIGURE 7.2   Standard Chartered: a balanced approach to development

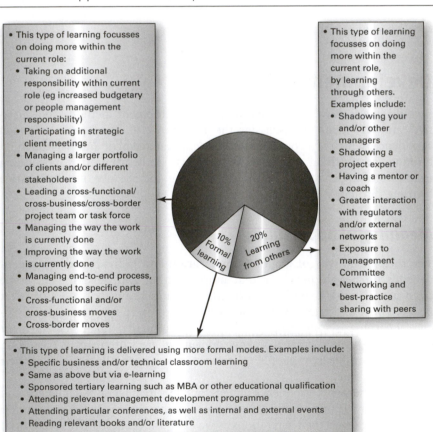

- This type of learning focusses on doing more within the current role:
  - Taking on additional responsibility within current role (eg increased budgetary or people management responsibility)
  - Participating in strategic client meetings
  - Managing a larger portfolio of clients and/or different stakeholders
  - Leading a cross-functional/cross-business/cross-border project team or task force
  - Managing the way the work is currently done
  - Improving the way the work is currently done
  - Managing end-to-end process, as opposed to specific parts
  - Cross-functional and/or cross-business moves
  - Cross-border moves

- This type of learning focusses on doing more within the current role, by learning through others. Examples include:
  - Shadowing your and/or other managers
  - Shadowing a project expert
  - Having a mentor or a coach
  - Greater interaction with regulators and/or external networks
  - Exposure to management Committee
  - Networking and best-practice sharing with peers

10% Formal learning

20% Learning from others

- This type of learning is delivered using more formal modes. Examples include:
  - Specific business and/or technical classroom learning
  - Same as above but via e-learning
  - Sponsored tertiary learning such as MBA or other educational qualification
  - Attending relevant management development programme
  - Attending particular conferences, as well as internal and external events
  - Reading relevant books and/or literature

Reproduced by permission of Standard Chartered Bank

The value of training

Importantly, an emphasis on development by experience should not eliminate training but should encourage a more targeted approach so that it is prioritized appropriately around business and individual needs.

Traditionally, it is often difficult to get the balance right between training the individual wants and training the organization needs. McDonald's is one organization that has achieved this balance and, as David Fairhurst, senior vice-president of McDonald's UK, puts it, 'has established training as part of its DNA'.

As with front-line service jobs generally, the McDonald's workforce is largely a transient one and more than half their employees are younger than 21. Working at McDonald's was generally held to be a dead-end job and the term 'McJob' came to be used to refer to just that: a dead-end job. McDonald's challenged this perception through its training strategy and, as research by Leeds Metropolitan University shows, more than half the McDonald's workforce leaves the company with better qualifications than when they joined. 'McJobs' are now perceived as a means of social mobility that enable McDonald's employees to go on to a successful career. Moreover, not everyone leaves. Many progress within the organization and McDonald's believes firmly in growing its own talent. Steve Easterbrook, UK chief executive and CEO of McDonald's Northern Europe, is a prime example, having joined them in the finance department in 1993.

McDonald's training offers something to benefit all employees, from people who are illiterate to PhD students. The benefits to the business are significant. The reputation of the training helps attract applicants, which makes recruitment easier and less costly. It reduces both the cost and time of initial training of new employees, leading to people being more effective more quickly. The company benefits from having engaged, well-qualified employees who remain advocates and enthusiasts for McDonald's after they have left.

The McDonald's approach has been to integrate training into its business philosophy, using it to help build its brand 'from the inside out' by providing an employment experience that enables it to attract the best talent in the marketplace and grow its own leaders.

Not all training must link to your integrated talent management system, but it is important to identify some targeted programmes that will reinforce your messages as well as help people develop their capabilities.

The value of coaching and mentoring

'Coaching and mentoring are about enhancing and developing the performance of the individual; their value being as a way of learning that is highly personal and flexible. They can be tailored at one and the same time to the needs of the individual and of the organization. They are about investing in the individual. A defining characteristic is that they are a one-to-one learning processes. There is a coach who may be a more senior executive, an outside consultant or a peer within the organization, and there is a learner. Generally the relationship involves an encouragement for the learner to discuss issues and identify problems and solutions for themselves, with a minimum of direction. However, the process can cover a wide range of uses and techniques.'[7]

Executive coaching and mentoring, ie coaching delivered by a qualified coach who is probably external to the organization, are widely and successfully used for development, and are especially effective for accelerating development.

The techniques and skills required of an executive coach are different from those needed for a coaching style of management or for peer coaching. As it is this coaching style that I refer to mainly in this book, it is appropriate to flag up particular uses of coaching that support talent management:

1 Coaching and mentoring may be used at any level within organizations, right up to the department head or chief executive. Executive coaching is commonly arranged for senior people to keep up with change, to reinvigorate a business and to support executives when they have been promoted – especially when this is to a more strategic role, perhaps with people management or strategic responsibilities for the first time.

2 Coaching can be a liberating stimulus to strategic ideas for the top executive whose status would be damaged by throwing out mad ideas among colleagues in the hope that one in a hundred is a winner. It often fills a gap in personal development and provides a sounding board for senior people who may not have anyone within their organizations with whom to discuss certain management issues.

3 While the non-directive coaching model, which facilitates the learner to arrive at their own solutions, is prevalent for most coaching, a different model seems to be emerging for coaching at senior levels. This model can best be described as a cross between non-directive coaching and consultancy advice. In this case, the coach may offer ideas and solutions, or input their expertise and experience. This 'advisory coaching', as I refer to it, is likely to increase over the next few years to support senior managers in embracing the new leadership models identified in Chapter 2, and perhaps also unlearn the old.

4 Coaching is also used to support training. Studies show that as few as 8 to 12 per cent of those who attend training translate new skills into measurable performance improvement.[8] The principal cause of this failure lies in the lack of follow-up, reinforcement or support: the trainee goes 'off site', learns and then returns to the day-to-day pressures of their role, where they often find it hard to apply what they have learnt. It has been shown that the effectiveness of training is significantly enhanced when it is followed up and supported by coaching.

As with the point made about training, the most successful approaches embed coaching into the philosophy of the business. The BBC case study at the end of this chapter is an example of this, as is the KPMG case study in Chapter 9.

Recent surveys, including the 2009 global coaching survey by Frank Bresser Consulting, show that coaching is now part of the mainstream of people management and widely and successfully used as a business tool in 28 countries (of these 14 are European). According to Bresser, there are about 43,000 to 44,000 business coaches operating in the world. Europe counts 18,000 business coaches and is the continent with the highest number. However, this is not evenly distributed: the UK and Germany, with 20 per cent of the European population, comprise around 70 per cent of all business coaches on the continent. Bresser's survey points to the importance of coaching, and suggests it will be an increasingly important development method.[9]

LEARNING POINTS

- Organizations compete through strengths in core capabilities and by discerning and then exploiting future opportunities. This means having people doing what they do best and doing it better and learning to do what will be required in the future.

- Capabilities are the cornerstone of an integrated talent management system, which offers a range of options for people to assess their strengths and preferences and then follows through on their development. Consistency of use helps build skills and understanding, and binds people through a common language and common philosophies.

- Assessment processes that start someone on their development journey encourage a culture of continuous learning and adaptability, and help managers develop people management skills. Building knowledge of behavioural capabilities through these processes gives the individual and the organization greater insight and understanding of what someone does best, and the capabilities to leverage when planning job opportunities. This helps achieve flexibility and positions people to create and take advantage of change.

- Achieving this level of flexibility in the workforce requires more than taking a note of who has which skills. It also requires a mindset that values people for their strengths and preferences, seeks to understand their aspirations and is prepared to take a risk with someone and offer them an accelerated career path or an opportunity they may not have the exact experience for. Consistency of message as well as practice is important.

Burson-Marsteller case study

Burson-Marsteller (B-M) is a leading global public relations and communications firm. It provides clients with advice and programme development across the spectrum of public relations, public affairs, digital media and, advertising, and other communications services. Its clients are global companies, industry associations, professional services firms, governments and other large organizations.

B-M has a highly developed and sophisticated use of new media technologies, such as its own internal version of YouTube and its own social networking sites, which enable people to interact with others and learn. For example, people can deepen their understanding of the firm's competencies by looking up anecdotes posted by others or by accessing videos of the firm's leaders talking about a competency and their experience of using it. People can also view videos of colleagues in different parts of the world discussing their use of the firm's competencies, which give fascinating insights into how people interpret them in different cultural contexts. The social networking sites bring people together from across the world to share experiences, knowledge and understanding. B-M sees new media technologies as offering outstanding possibilities for creating 'one company' – a virtual company.

B-M Source is a discussion forum where people can work together on a project or ask for help on some work. People can also post their profiles on the site and create networks around different topics or problems. These are proving to be an effective way of bringing people together and creating a culture of teamwork and collaboration.

B-M has also developed formal online learning programmes. At first these were on an open platform, but take-up and effectiveness have increased significantly since they have been linked into B-M's people processes and satisfactory completion has been acknowledged through a certification process. Paul Herrick, B-M's HR director for EMEA, believes the recognition attached to completion is important, as people do not otherwise perceive it as worth their time and effort. Herrick also measures effectiveness by obtaining feedback from participants and collecting statistics, such as viewing rates of videos and uptake of programmes.

Herrick believes that the success of B-M's social networking and online learning is both a consequence and a driver of B-M's culture of reaching out and being responsive to each other.

B-M's talent review process starts with a definition of the personal characteristics important for the growth of the business. People who meet these characteristics are offered a three-month assignment in a different country. This gives them an opportunity to experience a different culture and ways of doing things, as well as develop their understanding of B-M and gain deeper insights into some of B-M's clients, many of whom are global organizations. In fact, participants retain their home clients and work with them in the other location. Herrick has evidence that participation on this programme leads to higher engagement levels and company loyalty from those involved.

Participants have to apply for the assignment, making both a business and a personal case for their suitability and, importantly, for what they would gain from the experience and how they would follow it up. To be accepted on the programme, people have to be recognized as high performers and must have sustained this level of performance for at least two years. They must also have the support of their line manager. Some applicants are unsuccessful, but the reasons for rejection are explained to them and they are given guidance to enable them to apply again. Main aims of this initiative, which is a formally structured learning programme, are to build a sense of community globally across B-M, as well as give an outstanding development opportunity to high performers. While people are on assignment, and on their return, they are expected to spread their learning and share experiences with others through B-M's social networking sites.

LEARNING POINT

- This case study illustrates the benefits of using new technologies to promote global consistency and build a global identity. It shows an integrated approach to development through the link between competencies, new technologies, talent reviews and development opportunities.

BBC case study

The BBC's journalism group is responsible for all the BBC's news and current affairs output on television, radio and online. The BBC College of Journalism was formed in 2005 and is responsible for the design and delivery of learning and training to all BBC journalists in the UK and around the world. It teaches every aspect of journalism: craft skills like writing and storytelling; the technical skills required to operate in a digital, multi-platform world; social media and the web; and ethics, values and law. The learning is delivered through a wide variety of face-to-face training, one-to-one coaching, a programme of events and an extensive website. All learning interventions are guided by the BBC's five editorial values: truth and accuracy; impartiality; independence; public interest; accountability to audiences.

The BBC has always lived under the uncertainty of periodic debate over the licence fee but there is now additional uncertainty from the general business environment, especially the constantly evolving impact of new technologies. As a result, it is difficult to predict what the BBC's television, radio and online news departments will look like in the future. How will they be structured? What demarcation lines if any will there be between the different media or different locations? Will the programmes with the biggest following or influence be on television or online? What changes will be required as the licence debate continues? What will happen if the BBC's funding is reduced? What external partnerships might the BBC form? It may be hard to answer these questions now but it is possible to predict that, whatever the answers, the BBC will be required to do more with less, there will be more sharing between the World Service, television and radio and the news website; there is also likely to be more collaboration, with staff increasingly required to work across different media. So it may not yet be possible to formulate the BBC's long-term strategy but it is possible to determine the capabilities that will be required in the long term, and given the numbers involved – there are 8,000 employees across these departments – a range of training, coaching and online learning initiatives has been put in place to enable people to start developing these capabilities. These initiatives also aim to change perceptions about career paths and what are regarded as the most prestigious assignments, so that people will recognize the value of, say, building up an online following as a way of reaching a big audience.

Fiona Anderson (editor, coaching) at the College of Journalism runs coaching programmes in London, internationally and around the BBC centres producing dedicated news and current affairs output across the UK. Her coaching programmes, run for freelancers as well as staff, cover writing, presentation and voice. She has adapted the focus of the coaching over the years to keep pace with change, and one of her main concerns now is to develop a multi-skilled culture, where people are able to switch confidently from presenting on world television to domestic networks, from regional breakfast television to a late-night broadcast, or to radio news, or to writing for online. The skills required for each are different and require considerable preparation and training. The college tries to track each journalist and prepares them for different challenges, and helps them build their skills incrementally.

Anderson also uses the College of Journalism website extensively in training. It is a learning site 'for BBC journalists, by BBC journalists', which has now been made freely available to all UK web users at www.bbc.co.uk/journalism. The website contains a huge amount of content from leading journalists offering an unequalled opportunity for people to learn from each other and to grow. The site also offers staff opportunities to write news pieces and request feedback. Content is presented in a variety of ways – interactive exercises, podcasts, videos, reading materials – enabling people to choose methods that best suit their learning preferences.

One of the main principles behind the site, its content and its design is to be for journalists who are in a hurry but who feel they do not know enough about something. It is just-in-time learning. The site has recently been redesigned to make it more intelligent, so that it can offer users further suggestions of what will help or interest them, based on the searches they have made.

Most people access the site briefly, during the day, to find information to help them with something they are currently working on. Sometimes people spend 30 minutes or more on the site and work more intensively on a specific skill to help their development, for example to develop their writing skills. Events and discussion tend to engage news journalists most. Anderson links her coaching to the website by identifying appropriate online activities for people to use as follow-up.

As Anderson points out, people have always valued working at the BBC because it offers outstanding training. The College of Journalism certainly fulfils that remit.

The Pathfinder development programme is a strategic initiative, also supported by the College of Journalism, that gives people the opportunity to experience working in different media. It is a structured learning-by-experience initiative. For the first of these, 14 programme producers were assigned to work on programmes to bring them up to speed on all aspects of radio, television and online. Two producers were given the opportunity to work in a central planning team to work on multimedia, and four went to work in the bureaux in Delhi and Cairo, again to work across all media.

For the first Pathfinder programme, editors were asked to nominate candidates who best matched the criteria for participation. These criteria covered motivation, engagement, commitment and potential. In its second year of operation, places have been advertised internally for people to apply for the opportunity. Although nomination seemed the best way to get the programme going, the success of the first year meant they now had champions to encourage others and set the example. Applicants were asked to respond to questions that included: Why should we give this opportunity to you? What would you want to take back to your home programme? What do you bring to the department? The aims of the application procedure were to ensure that people understood the context and thought about what they would contribute and how it would benefit them. The standard among the applicants was high and 26 people were selected.

Rejected candidates received detailed feedback and were given support on action that would help them match the criteria better next time. Line managers were involved in this and were expected to reinforce the messages as well as support their staff towards being able to match the criteria in future.

One of the challenges for Sara Beck, who organizes the Pathfinder initiative, is to ensure that participants are given the opportunity to use their new skills when they return to their home department. The management team plays a key role here in making it clear to editors that it is in their interest to produce material for multimedia. Within one month of their return, participants are expected to research and produce multimedia pieces. A debrief between the participant, their editor and Beck following the exercise is set up to encourage this. While still attached to a home department, participants are regarded as a flexible resource and editors or producers can ask for someone for an assignment because of their new multimedia skills.

Coaching has become a powerful instrument for achieving change and for helping people develop at the BBC, and Anderson's team has grown as a result. Her colleague, Tony Worgan, has taken on the role of coaching line managers at the BBC's local radio stations and is passionate about people managing their talent in order to make the BBC's output better. Worgan devotes two-thirds of his time to line managers. He has regular conversations with them to discuss what they are doing and to provide additional support and follow-up where they need it. The start of the line manager programme is a two-day coaching course, followed by a conference call about six to eight weeks afterwards and then a follow-up day some three to four months later. This tends to be the defining moment when you can see whether someone is going to be a successful manager-coach; but Anderson and Worgan find that the training for coaching always results in increased self-awareness, so everyone benefits from it. As a result of Worgan's work, commercial radio managers are now running sessions each week to listen, together with staff, to their broadcast, to give them feedback and to coach them. Worgan has succeeded in embedding coaching as a key part of the role of a radio managing editor. Anderson explains that a request for coaching must be supported by a line manager who must also brief the learner beforehand to agree coaching objectives. They must also carry out a debrief afterwards and follow through with the person in applying what they have learned.

Anderson manages a business-focused relationship with line managers, discussing with them what they are trying to achieve and how coaching fits into the BBC's overall objectives. She also works with them to encourage them to notice change and praise it, to encourage a virtuous circle of change. Each line manager has a responsibility to improve the performance of their team members, and their own performance measures include their role to develop staff and give them feedback.

LEARNING POINT

- This case study describes a development initiative aimed at long-term strategic change. It illustrates a key point of talent management: that even without knowing all aspects of the long-term strategy, it is still possible to identify future technical and behavioural capabilities and set in place development that benefits everyone now, while establishing the flexibility to adapt to change. The programme achieves clear cultural aims as well as professional ones and involves fair, consistent assessment criteria together with that all-important follow-through. Top management and individual line managers support it and give individuals the recognition that is essential to its success and to ensuring its future uptake.

References

1 Purcell, J *et al* (2003) *Understanding the People and Performance Link: Unlocking the Black Box*, CIPD, London
2 Roberts, G (1999) *Recruitment and Selection: a competency approach*, CIPD, London
3 Paton, N (2006) Custom designed, *HR Today, Saturday Guardian*, 1 April
4 http://www.thescalagroup.co.uk/resources1.html
5 Harter, J K *et al* (2006) Gallup Q12 Meta-Analysis
6 http://www.cipd.co.uk/subjects/recruitmen/general/_recruitment_summary.htm
7 Caplan, J (2003) *Coaching for the Future: How smart companies use coaching and mentoring*, CIPD
8 Skiffington, S and Zeus, P (1999) What is executive coaching?, *Management Today*, November
9 Frank Bresser Consulting (2009) *Global coaching survey, executive summary*: http://www.frank-bresser-consulting.com/globalcoachingsurvey09-executivesummary.pdf

Deployment

08

FIGURE 8.1 Deployment

The most common approach to succession planning is to focus on identifying one or more successors for key posts (or groups of similar key posts) and plan career moves and/or development activities for these successors. The objective is to anticipate needs and have at least one possible successor ready to step into a role when it becomes available. Planned successors may be ready to do the job now or they may need further development or have the long-term potential.

Many businesses classify people into 'talent pools' that group those with similar profiles and, therefore, similar development needs. One of the most typical contains employees judged to have the potential for further management and leadership responsibility. Talent pools, in these cases, provide a structured and focused approach to the development of people within them to realize their potential more quickly. They also help concentrate the time and attention of line management, and use the development budget where it will bring the greatest return for the business.

Another approach to 'talent pools' is one that focuses on identifying people who are regarded as pivotal talent. These are people who can make a material difference to your business and whose skills or performance will make you better than your rivals. This also means that the business must identify its pivotal roles. The aim here is again to optimize investment in developing people to bring the greatest business return.

The purpose of succession planning has traditionally been to prepare the organization now for anticipated changes, and approaches have generally been crafted around this purpose. But what of the 'new world' organization where changes are harder to foresee?

The approach to succession planning that I propose in this chapter addresses all these objectives and suggests a basic process that stands up to the pace and uncertainties of business life today. Importantly, it is a devolved process that emphasizes that everyone is important to the organization. Achieving this requires a dynamic succession planning process that informs your people processes and business strategies and that filters through into everyone's development plans. This vitally aligns organization and individual development.

I will explain my approach through the ABC Engineering case study, picking this up from Chapters 4 and 7. I will use this case study to go through the key elements of a succession planning process but will also bring in other examples that illustrate different methods and approaches.

Reasons for developing a succession plan

Every organization needs to plan for the long term. Succession planning must be relevant to the business and its corporate values. Equally, it must also be relevant to individuals.

At first, we set out to do succession planning at ABC in a traditional way by focusing on people for future leadership posts. However, early on we realized that this wouldn't work in this culture; in addition, there were some people across all levels – executives, managers, technicians – who had unique experience and very scarce skills. Developing a traditional leadership pipeline would not address these critical business continuity issues below the top team. We therefore needed to have a more holistic process and match people with critical roles, scarce skills and also with potential to grow and develop other skills. We therefore sought to design a dynamic process that would filter through to everyone and that would also inform the firm's people processes and business strategies.

The process we designed achieved three main outcomes:

- A snapshot of people able to cover or move into the two top-tier management roles. This snapshot enabled us to identify shortages and vulnerabilities so as to plan recruitment and internal development to overcome these. We also identified pivotal talent: that is, those people who made a difference to the business. At ABC, people regarded as pivotal had specialist knowledge and experience vital to the business and not easy to replicate.

- The opportunity for people to actively pursue a personal development plan that aligned their aspirations with the development of the business. This helped create several talent pipelines to deal with the considerable technical, environmental and leadership challenges the business faced. It also aimed to help people realize their potential. This was the more unusual element to the process as it covered all management, technical and specialist staff.

- Input into a resourcing strategy and a learning and development strategy. The information we generated through this process provided the main input into these strategies but also provided input into the firm's business strategies.

The following are the unique stages of this dynamic succession planning process, and I will follow them to set out my ideas:

1 Reasons for developing a succession plan and its aims.
2 Collect data on roles, capabilities and organizational requirements.
3 Collect data on individuals.
4 Talent pools and classifications, and talent review conversations.
5 Analyse the data collected to identify resourcing and learning and development requirements and any business improvements that have emerged.
6 Review and update the plan regularly and use it to keep track of people and their development.

The purpose and aims of a succession plan

Our remit at ABC was to produce a plan for the firm's remuneration committee, to show that the business had successors in place to fill top management posts and key roles, and also to ensure business continuity. We needed to identify these key roles but we also set out to design a process that would serve a purpose beyond that of the remuneration committee and would align with the firm's vision, values, and business strategies, especially its talent management strategies.

The first step in the process was to expand on why we needed succession planning and what it should achieve. To do this, we spent a considerable amount of time 'listening to the business' – following the process set out in Appendix A and that we had first applied to develop the talent strategy.

These conversations confirmed that future business success would demand sophisticated leadership, project management and relationship building skills, which would be just as important as highly specialized technical knowledge. These capabilities were already part of the talent management programme.

Wendy Hirsh, a leading authority on the subject, believes succession planning often enables people to distinguish the main functions of the business –

for example, service delivery and marketing – and identify generic skills patterns, such as project management skills that are required for a range of different posts.[1] This certainly reflects our experience at ABC, where our conversations at this first stage led to us designing a process that, instead of focusing on job functions, would influence the skills development required for the future. These conversations also led to us interpreting the requirement for a pipeline of people to fill key posts as being a process to include everyone. This aligned well with the chief executive's vision expressed through his 'Two dots' philosophy as well as with the organization's value of fairness.

Collect data on roles, capabilities and organizational requirements

Succession planning essentially involves collecting data on people and roles, matching the two and analysing the gaps.

At ABC we needed data on present roles, and also needed to reflect the capabilities required for the future. Much of this data was already available. Job descriptions, the organization chart, the firm's budget and its business plan were major sources. Future capabilities had been previously identified through the talent management strategy. From this data gathering we were able to identify:

- Roles to be covered by the plan (we covered the top two of the three management tiers).
- Job clusters by capabilities, required experience, etc.
- Functional and situational experience required for each, especially the most senior roles. Functional can be divided into scarce and/or critical skills, complex skills requiring long training periods, and possible skills required for the future. Situational may be multicultural fluency, entrepreneurial skills, leading significant change, international experience, etc.

Collect data on individuals

Succession processes are underpinned by having detailed information on people and the business. We achieved this by drawing up talent notes on everyone in each management tier. These summarized people's capability profile, career development aspirations and performance data. They also suggested development needs and career paths. We used these notes as a basis of discussion with every line manager. We got them thinking about roles now and in the future and also thinking about people's development. These detailed discussions helped to make line managers more comfortable and confident in their ability to talk to their own staff about development.

The questions we asked line managers were similar to those set out in Appendix A, starting with current and future business and environmental challenges and the implications of these in terms of skill sets and capabilities. We then extended the questioning to ask managers to identify successors to their own roles and those of the people in the next management tier. Although we discussed job functions, we focused more on capabilities. Through our line of questioning, line managers identified the experience, learning and training that people would require. We also asked line managers about themselves, their aspirations, future career moves and the experience or learning they needed. We asked whom they regarded as possible successors to their boss, and what special skills and experience their boss had that would be hard to replicate.

By the end of these conversations, we had produced draft talent notes for all managers, as well as a spreadsheet identifying those who would be able to move into the tiers covered by the succession plan and the development they required. The talent notes also suggested a three-stage development plan for each person (see Chapter 7): the stretch/challenge in the current role and two career moves beyond that. Against each stage, there were also development suggestions. Importantly, we had encouraged managers to identify successors for roles and for skills sets from across the organization. We also asked them in which other parts of the business their staff could potentially work. This was important to encouraging cross-functional career moves and opening career paths.

These talent notes established vital links between individuals' development plans, their aspirations, their capability strengths, their performance and business needs. The idea of this was to facilitate conversations and not be prescriptive.

Following these conversations, we sent a copy of each talent note to both the line manager and the individual to use in their forthcoming performance appraisal discussions and to form the basis of development planning.

One of the most valuable results gained from these conversations was that they had served as mini coaching sessions for line managers, who then held similar conversations with their staff. When we reviewed the process at a later stage, it was clear that these conversations and the talent notes had been well received.

Conversations around talent notes helped line managers develop a talent mindset, as they emphasized the importance of:

- future-focused thinking on the business challenges that lie ahead;
- providing meaningful opportunity to their employees;
- understanding people's aspirations and aligning these with organizational needs;
- building on people's strengths and preferences.

It was through these talent notes that we ensured that the succession plan was a dynamic one and followed through. This also ensured that the people nominated for senior roles in the short or long term received appropriate development, while at the same time giving everyone development opportunities that were right for them.

Once the first talent notes had been compiled, they could be maintained and also extended to those staff at junior and entry levels by adapting internal social networking technologies. This enables people to compile internal CVs providing information to be used, perhaps confidentially, to populate their talent notes, but that they can also use internally for social networking or information sharing. This lessens the HR workload and gives control and ownership to the individual. It also makes the process more user friendly and relevant, which makes it more likely people will follow it.

According to Hirsh, this devolved model where the same processes and philosophies are cascaded through the business are especially common in large organizations.[2] She points out, however, that few successfully sustain it, usually because it is not really seen as a high priority and not adequately facilitated by HR. From my experience, the first time of undertaking succession planning is labour-intensive but well worth the effort. At ABC, for example, our succession plan provided a valuable snapshot of organizational health, and at the same time achieved additional benefits, perhaps the two most significant being to put long-term development firmly on the map and to impart to line managers the skills for holding conversations about aspirations and development.

Standard Chartered uses a devolved succession planning process that they have been maintaining and refining over several years. In Chapter 2, I referred to the company's process whereby each of the CEO's direct reports present their strategic people agenda to him. As part of this, there is a second discussion about succession planning. In this way, the CEO reviews the strength and experience of the leadership team and pipeline for the bank. As discussions with these direct reports progress, they inevitably spill over and raise questions about the broader context of business plans and strategies. They also cover what someone brings to a role and how to leverage this to the benefit of the business.

The bank's succession plan extends through the senior and middle management levels. Line managers classify their people annually for potential. These classifications are used to track people to ensure that they receive the right development and to check their progress through the organization in comparison with their peers.

Each employee in the banded levels covered by the succession planning process has access to a talent profile, which they can update annually. This includes setting out their aspirations and development actions as well as performance data.

Each business head compiles a succession plan for their area and all business heads then come together with their teams to share information and discuss the people on the plan. These discussions look at each person and whether their strengths are being leveraged, and make sure they are being given the right development opportunities. They are a valuable way to create the right conversations and mindsets. This process and these conversations cascade through each area of the bank.

Geraldine Haley, group head of leadership effectiveness and succession, takes a macro-level view of the succession plan, checking the quality of the data, for instance, to ensure it reflects the bank's diversity agenda, that the bank has the right flow of people through the talent pipelines, that it is on track to meet the bank's strategic goals. This strategic overview is reported, twice a year, to the board nomination committee and group management committee. This gives external endorsement and external critical assessment of the succession planning process, and its related talent agenda.

Haley ensures this plan is live and not something static that sits in a drawer. Every two weeks, she chairs a 'resourcing call' with the heads of HR of each business unit to discuss changes coming up in the organization, how these present opportunities to refresh planning and whether there is a need to look at external hiring.

Reference is made to the succession plan when a job opportunity arises. Sometimes appointments are made solely by reference to the plan. This is possible because, to be on the plan, the individual will already have been considered carefully and by a wide range of people. Information on people comes from a variety of sources, which include data such as performance data over an extended period, engagement survey data, and also opinion. Haley emphasizes, however, that appointments are made by knowing the person and by having someone who knows them well to sponsor them. She stresses that they are both relationship based and data driven when it comes to making internal selection decisions.

In making any appointment, Standard Chartered works to ensure that it is an objective and data-driven decision. The internal recruitment process involves the recruiting line manager, one other senior manager and HR. When they consider someone for possible future positions they hold conversations around the people, their strengths, skills and aspirations: what they could do next, what they are interested in, who supports them, if they have a mentor or coach. The succession plan and talent profiles are used. The bank also considers information on employee strengths and engagement scores.

On the whole, Standard Chartered views talent classifications and succession planning data as a snapshot in time that needs to be regularly reviewed and updated, as well as acted upon. It is now starting to share talent classifications with people and is encouraging line managers to have conversations with their people about these.

Haley and her team also check plans at a senior leadership level to identify who is not on the plan and why. This may be because the person is coming up for retirement or they are new in a job. Occasionally it indicates a performance problem.

As with ABC Engineering, Standard Chartered has crafted a process that aligns with vision, values and wider business strategy. HR people actively drive and facilitate the process, which has been designed with the line manager firmly in mind. You may care to note also how at ABC we integrated succession planning closely with our talent processes.

The focus at Standard Chartered is slightly different, reflecting the size and global reach of the organization. Here it is interesting to note that Jolene Chen, group head of resourcing, learning and talent development, and her team work with the local HR business and country relationship managers, who then maintain the process through their relationships with line managers.

Talent pools and classifications; talent review conversations

Why do you want talent pools or classifications and what will you do with them? Talent considerations are likely to be different for different organizations depending on size and activities. At ABC Engineering, we drew up classifications so that we could track that the people who were ready for the next move or for stretch and challenge, or who needed more support, received the development, experience and promotion they needed. Our approach, especially through the talent notes, was essentially to provide individual opportunity and development in such a way that this naturally took care of the high performers and those with higher potential and aspiration. I believe these approaches also took account of people who at different stages, and for different reasons, would be critical to business performance.

Paul Herrick at Burson-Marsteller similarly tries to avoid the term 'high potential', believing it is often misused. Instead, B-M have identified what is known as 'six for six': that is, each person has to satisfy each of the six characteristics at their level. The aim is to develop people to be part of a pool of excellence from which the leaders and key roles will be recruited. Examples of these characteristics are: a track record for winning new business; has acted as mentor to others and can describe to others what this involved and the benefits gained; business acumen as demonstrated through depth of understanding of the business and what it is about. As with other professional firms, and in the ABC Engineering example, this is not about succession planning in the sense of identifying people who could perform a particular role, neither is it about identifying leaders; rather it is about providing outstanding development for people so that they develop the skills sets and capabilities required for the future success of the business, and also to match their own aspirations.

At B-M, towards the end of the last quarter of the year, business objectives are cascaded through the organization, so that people are clear about the main performance areas for the following year and set their objectives in line with them. Those who meet the criteria for being in the top pool of talent are then tracked. Herrick and the chief executive check that their performance objectives contain clear, challenging and stretching measures.

While learning and development are especially important for everyone at B-M, particular attention is taken to ensure that people in the top talent pool follow a challenging learning path programme. Line managers are required to discuss learning interventions with the individual to encourage them to reflect on what they have learned and how they can apply this learning. Herrick and the person's line manager identify reading materials for the person, who is also brought into discussions about an element of the firm's business strategy. They are expected to gain a deep understanding of the strategy, its implications and any possible alternatives. They are expected to develop ideas about its implementation, challenging the CEO on aspects of it, being challenged in turn, and championing its implementation. People in the top talent pool have also worked on a joint project around corporate responsibility, which is a major business area on which B-M advises clients.

It is interesting to note from this example the link created between succession planning and performance appraisal and the role of the line manager, the emphasis on development by experience, and especially how this includes exposing someone to the firm's overall business strategy. B-M's method is built around the business need to identify potential around capabilities rather than job functions.

Nine-box matrix

The most commonly used system of classifying people is through the performance and potential matrix or nine-box matrix, or a variant of this. This is a grid with which you plot employees based on their performance ranking and their potential for advancement. Based on a method originally developed by McKinsey, this is essentially a convenient way of taking a macro view of performance and potential across the organization. The main problem with it is achieving consistency of performance and potential classifications across the organization. On the other hand, having discussions around it can help achieve this consistency, as is the case at Bekaert who have developed a relatively straightforward version of the matrix.

Bekaert holds performance reviews twice yearly, using a five-point rating scale that feeds into the talent reviews. The performance review discussion covers the individual's career development aspirations and fields of interest, as well performance; and this is documented.

Bekaert uses the nine-box matrix for this review and every manager above a certain job evaluation classification is assigned to one of the boxes on the matrix. The sponsoring line manager (the person to whom the individual

FIGURE 8.2   Example of the nine-box matrix

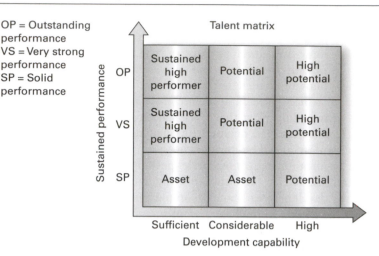

Developed by Bernard Vanhecke, Bekaert and reproduced with permission

reports) will discuss the level of classification they want to assign someone with their own line manager and with their HR manager. All managers in each unit will then meet together, for one day, to discuss each person in the matrix, their performance levels and their potential. The process is then taken to executive committee level, whose focus is on the senior managers and who discuss those capable of filling the top 100 jobs in the organization.

The talent review process brings many benefits. It encourages a team approach to identifying potential and discussing talent. This helps overcome problems of line managers wanting to hold on to good people and it also means that individuals are not necessarily reliant on one person to sponsor them. This process also emphasizes the importance of encouraging and supporting individual development. Once the executive committee approves the talent plan, the line manager is required to identify a personal development plan for the individual and is responsible for ensuring it is carried out; but it is HR's role to facilitate and challenge. As mentioned previously, Bekaert believes strongly in development through experience.

People know about this process and through conversations with their line manager will understand how their performance is perceived in the organization. The classifications are used for workforce planning and control, rather than as a way of boxing people or labelling them. They are also intended to be fluid, allowing movement in and out of the boxes and the roles on the succession plan, according to business and other changes.

Although this talent review process is globally run for the senior management levels, some of Bekaert's business units extend it to everyone in their unit. The process itself confers strategic and team-building benefits through bringing senior managers together as a team to review the talent flow in and out of the business. When you are confronted, for argument's sake, with all your unit managers in the same left-hand corner box, you realize that you will have future succession problems and that you need to address them. The process focuses senior management on preparing for the next 10 to 20 years. It does not identify business critical posts, as all positions in the organization are interconnected and it is difficult to say that one post is more critical than another.

This talent review process links into the business planning cycle, which is a three-year rolling plan that covers both organization and people. It precedes the business plan review, so that plans are made with reference to the people in place and their capabilities.

Similarly to Standard Chartered, Bekaert appoints people to senior level internal vacancies when they know from the talent review process that the person is suitable. There will be an interview but this is generally more about interesting the person in the role than in assessing their suitability. This can lead those who are excluded from consideration to feel frustrated, but this disadvantage is outweighed by the advantages of bringing together experienced people who know both the business and the people well and of having them take responsibility for the decision.

Purshouse believes that Bekaert is a very special place, offering excellent opportunity. He himself is an example of this; originally from the UK, he has had an international career with the company. He feels the company demands a lot from its people but allows them considerable latitude to get on with their jobs. He believes people are genuinely helpful and cooperative.

Bekaert's process of succession planning and talent reviews, similarly to Standard Chartered, is a key process for achieving global consistency. Both organizations use data and opinion in equal measure, and as we saw in Chapter 5 on assessment, Bekaert's use of assessment and development centres provides additional information for the organization, as well as development support for the individual. All organizations in the examples emphasize development by experience and this is an important underpinning of the talent review conversations, which seek to ensure that people receive not just the appropriate classification but also the appropriate development and support.

I have sought to consider the use of talent classifications and what you do with them by giving examples of different kinds of organizations with different needs. In large, global organizations, or those comprising different businesses, such as Standard Chartered, Bekaert or GMG (see Chapter 3), the emphasis is best placed on people who are in mid career and may rise to be the future business leaders. In these cases, the succession planning model will likely focus on these levels but will encourage a similar, devolved process through the individual businesses. The bright and ambitious graduates of firms such as Burson-Marsteller cannot all reach the top levels. While these firms can still offer opportunity and career development to those who will not reach director or partner level, many prefer to seek leadership roles elsewhere. This means that career paths need to be well mapped, what is required at each stage must be clearly identified and communicated, and people need to be given appropriate support. This requires identifying leadership potential at an earlier stage than might be the case in, say, a large industrial conglomerate. It is generally preferable in professional services firms to populate the senior levels of the organization mostly from within, to provide client continuity. The reverse might be true, however, in some corporations that offer their customers the latest technology and services. They often need complex organizational structures and the ability to innovate will be highly prized. As a result, they are likely to be constantly searching for external talent, even at senior levels, and are also likely to search worldwide to find it. In these businesses, talent pools are likely to focus on technical and behavioural capabilities, and provide a strong interface with the external resourcing programme. ABC Engineering is one such example and the link with external resourcing is discussed in the next section. Yet another scenario is provided by organizations in retailing and hospitality, for example, that experience high staff turnover. Here succession planning is likely to focus on a small core of people and roles where they wish to build long-term commitment and loyalty.

In summary, therefore, the use of talent pools and talent classifications can be useful to provide macro-level control so that HR and senior management have information for the purposes of workforce planning and development. Mavericks are often valuable and, in the new world organization, it is essential to keep these classifications under constant review to be sure that they enable the organization to adapt to change immediately. Using an approach that focuses on the capabilities the organization is likely to need for its future success can be beneficial here. Organizations that currently focus only on job roles should consider introducing this element into their succession planning.

Perhaps the greatest benefit of talent classifications is that they facilitate talent review conversations, which bring many benefits:

1 They create a talent mindset, making senior management aware of knowing people and developing them in line with the organization's requirements. It raises consciousness that the capabilities of the organization are an aggregation of the people within it.

2 They help achieve consistency in assessing performance and help people develop a common view of what makes for success and high performance.

3 They bring people to the notice of other parts of the business and result in better development plans.

4 They reduce the effects of silo working by creating synergies across divisions.

5 They often highlight business improvements or lead directors and line managers to challenge assumptions behind the business strategy.

6 They improve teamwork and understanding among peer levels.

7 They help the business define performance levels so that the value to the organization of steady contributors and high performers is clear. This should then enable line managers to have better conversations with people about how they are doing and what the future holds for them.

The most important part of this process is making sure people have the development that aligns their aspirations with those of the organization. As in the case study examples, a belief that development is about experience must be 'how we do things around here'. This is, of course, a key element of the talent mindset, where line managers recognize their responsibility to provide people with meaningful opportunity.

The role of the board of directors

Ensuring succession is a major responsibility of the board of directors or equivalent. Good corporate governance requires that non-executive directors ensure that the company has the resources, particularly money and people, sufficient to implement its strategy. Non-executive directors, therefore, have a major interest in the information generated by the succession plan and in ensuring that the business has the people to provide business continuity in a crisis and is sustainable in the long term. Non-executive directors also are generally on the remuneration committee and are responsible for the salaries and bonuses paid to the board.

GMG has developed an effective process for involving its directors and non-executive directors in succession planning. Two separate meetings about senior leadership development and succession planning are held every six months. One is the nominations committee consisting of all non-executive directors and chaired by the GMG chairperson. The other is the senior succession and leadership development committee chaired by the CEO. This has as its membership the CEOs/MDs of the businesses. It meets one month prior to the nominations committee. Carolyn Gray, GMG's HR director, is secretary to both committees. At these two-hour meetings, committee members review succession plans and discuss the 'rising stars' coming up through the different organizations that comprise the group. They have detailed and challenging conversations about these people, which also causes them to question and discuss different aspects of business strategy and direction, as well as policy and practice. In addition to ensuring there is an appropriate talent pipeline for future leadership positions, the nominations committee also discusses the development plans for each person, to ensure these will provide relevant experience to suit both the individual and the business. Gray believes that at GMG they have succeeded in introducing a rigour into their succession planning process that is often hard to achieve. Gray has sought to actively involve non-executive directors in the business as much as possible, in different ways to suit each individual and to enable the business to benefit from the particular strengths and experiences each brings. This might be lecturing on a topic or about an experience on the group's leadership programme; or bringing someone into a meeting with some members of staff. This involvement gives the non-executive directors insights into the business that enable them to engage more actively and more deeply in board discussions. GMG regards succession as a major area of potential business risk if it is not addressed appropriately.

Analyse the data collected

At ABC Engineering, we drew up a succession plan showing people who could cover roles on a contingency basis, as well as who could be ready in the near future and in the longer term. This plan was important to provide a snapshot of the organization to reveal any current risk.

However, we produced a parallel plan showing skills sets and capabilities rather than roles and who was already able to cover these, or could potentially do so with appropriate development. This gave a more accurate plan to prepare for long-term sustainability, which would depend more on people with the right capabilities than on 'filling shoes'.

A major purpose of any succession planning process is to identify organizational vulnerabilities as well as develop resourcing and learning and development plans. A powerful side product is its contribution to business improvements. At ABC Engineering, we drew up a report commenting on the issues that had arisen in the process. These related to the organization overall and each major division or business unit. This was discussed at board level, as part of corporate governance procedures.

Having a solid appreciation of organizational strengths and vulnerabilities for the immediate and longer term made it easy to create coherent external resourcing and learning and development strategies, addressing what we would do about these vulnerabilities. The latter was for everyone: those with high potential, those with scarce skills, those with potential skills. In identifying people who were able to cover certain skill needs, or technical areas, especially in the event of a short-term contingency, external suppliers and consultants were also included in the succession plan, not by naming individuals but with reference to their business as a source of potential cover. By implementing this we were able to mitigate the risk of not having people with the right skills, and this piece of the programme closed the loop on aligning individual and organizational requirements.

In global organizations or large conglomerates the succession planning emphasis is likely to be on the top leadership levels to ensure a pipeline of people who can fill future leadership roles. This has become increasingly necessary due to the shortages of leaders worldwide but it also reflects an increasing recognition shown through studies on employee engagement that an emphasis on growing your own leaders helps attract and retain people at all levels. However, it must always be kept in mind that the relative importance of certain capabilities might change rapidly in the 'new world' and this must be factored into the analysis.

Review and update the plan regularly

All the case study organizations have created a dynamic process around the basic requirement of succession planning, which is to ensure a suitable pipeline of people to meet future organizational needs. In each case, the succession process links back to performance management and facilitates conversations between line managers and their employees. Plans are also kept under constant review to ensure they keep up-to-date with change and to enable people to move in and out of talent classifications.

Succession planning must also feed into learning and development planning. At ABC Engineering, the nature of the organization and of the diverse specialties of the workforce meant that development needs were highly individualized. The common development link for people was provided through the behavioural capability framework. In organizations such as B-M and GMG, people who are identified as successors or who meet certain performance and potential criteria, whether through a formal talent classification or not, are offered a more structured programme.

LEARNING POINTS

- Organizations have a variety of needs for succession planning. For some this means identifying people to fill future leadership or other key roles. For others it means determining capabilities required for the future, often those critical to business success, and identifying the people who can potentially be developed to meet them.

- Use talent notes to facilitate line managers' conversations with staff about aspirations and development and to emphasize the importance of development by experience.

- Devolving succession planning so that the organization retains flexibility is important. Moreover, identifying critical or pivotal talent is becoming harder as roles become more interconnected and the pace of change rapidly creates different requirements.

- Developing your own leaders will always be crucial. This is partly because of global shortages, but also because promoting leaders from within leads to higher engagement levels as it demonstrates that individuals are valued.

- Hold regular talent review meetings among groups of line managers. This builds their skills and achieves consistency.
- Robust succession planning will identify people to fill future appointments; but it requires a good balance between data and judgement, both of which must come from multiple sources.

References

1 Hirsh, W (2000) Succession planning demystified, *Institute for Employment Studies*, report 372, October
2 *ibid*

Engagement

09

FIGURE 9.1   Engagement

Talent
Management

Realizing the value of talent in the organization requires an inclusive approach where everyone has a role in making talent management important. The CEO and top team set the direction and the tone, HR designs the strategy and provides the tools and practices, line managers deliver them and individuals take advantage of them. The talent strategy, systems and processes assist line managers, but they cannot work alone. Indeed, the way these practices are implemented by line managers has a greater impact on employee engagement than any of the intrinsic merits of the talent policies themselves. How people bring these practices to life is specific to the individuals and the organization; and because they can have a significant effect on employee behaviour and company culture, and because this is difficult to imitate, it can become a potential source of competitive advantage. In contrast, policies and practices can be copied, but advantage that is embedded in the very culture of an organization is hard to simulate.

In this chapter, I examine the role of the leaders of businesses in ensuring that talent management brings this competitive advantage to the organization. This is important to our overall understanding: it will help you identify leadership capabilities, plan leadership development, and know how to better support leaders in their roles. I have covered the critical role of line managers in delivering talent management throughout this book, but look at it again in the next chapter when I discuss how HR can support both the top team and the line. At the end of this chapter, I set out case studies from Standard Chartered and KPMG, showing their approach to leadership development.

What are the talent management responsibilities of the people at the top?

What must the people at the top do to promote a talent management approach? This can be illustrated by considering four key roles of the leadership team:

- espousing and promoting vision and values;
- creating strategy;
- implementing the strategy;
- managing the team.

While it is easy to list these roles, they have complicated interactions with each other and the management of people is both a specific role and represents the entire process itself. Figure 9.2 tries to capture these ideas. It shows vision and values informing strategy creation, which, in turn, leads on to its implementation. It illustrates how communication to and from the team takes place during each process. It also shows this two-way communication with the outside world of investors, business partners and financiers, at the level of vision and values. But while information from the outside world influences strategy, this is a one-way street. Finally it shows a different form of communication, through actions, as strategy is implemented.

FIGURE 9.2   Talent management responsibilities of people at the top

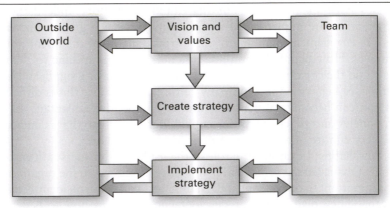

Espousing and promoting vision and values

As we discussed in Chapter 2, a devolved leadership model that creates shared vision, values and understanding is becoming the prevalent leadership model on which the organization thrives. This in no way diminishes the responsibilities and accountabilities of the top leadership. Rather it emphasizes that setting the tone and strategic direction requires behavioural capabilities that are at least different from, and perhaps also more complex than, those demanded of the 'command and control' model.

The starting point for leadership is the set of values that underpins what leaders do and how they do it. It informs their own behaviour, what they expect of colleagues and what they expect of the business. It feeds into the vision they have for the business, which leads on to goals and strategies, and influences how those are selected and carried out. Values are more than just ethics; they relate to which behaviours are regarded as important or, indeed, unacceptable. So a sales-driven organization is likely to give high importance to achieving sales but may also regard competition between sales executives as part of their value set. Another similar organization may take a completely contrary view that sales executives should work collaboratively, and it would be shocked by any tricks employed to win a sale at the expense of a colleague. These values will be fundamental to how each business operates and what strategies they select. For example, the competitive environment will probably seek to closely control price competition to prevent their own people driving down prices against each other, whereas the collaborative organization may be more able to aim for price leadership in the market, in the knowledge that prices will not be driven down by internal competition.

To some extent these company values may reflect personal values but that is not always the case. Instead of reaching within themselves for feelings the leaders may discuss approaches to business in a reasoned and analytical way so that there may be no contradiction between an introverted leader espousing a strongly customer-centred approach that focuses attention on the customer's needs before worrying about profitability.

Above all, as we saw in Chapter 2, these values will directly influence corporate culture and thence the business vision that is a key leadership role. The vision is the narrative of what the business is about: the story that inspires everyone and guides them along its broad direction. It enables the leader, but also others, to select goals and strategies that are aligned to the vision and values, that are consistent and all lead in the same direction.

As we have already identified, talent management strategy must align with vision and values, and with business strategy. This gives the people at the top a crucial role in determining values and living them in a way that drives and reinforces the principles of talent management.

Creating strategy

Senior leaders also have a critical role in determining the overall strategic direction of the business. In the new business environment this means seeking input from colleagues and subordinates; it means being able to create and spot change by making judgements between disparate views, and connections between superficially unrelated issues. Despite widely varied opinions about the key characteristics of leaders at the top, there is almost complete agreement by commentators that being forward-looking – envisioning exciting possibilities and enlisting others in a shared view of the future – is the attribute that most distinguishes leaders from non-leaders. In 2009 Kouzes and Posner surveyed tens of thousands of people and reported that 'No other quality showed such a dramatic difference between leader and colleague.'[1]

Wasserman's description of different levels of strategic thinking and development are helpful: 'Leaders on the front line must anticipate merely what comes after current projects wrap up. People at the next level of leadership should be looking several years into the future. And those [at the top levels] must focus on a horizon some 10 years distant.'[2] While we can debate the precise timing, the important point is that the top leadership team must set a vision and develop strategies that extend years into the future. This is not to say that these are set in stone; one of the aspects of strategic plans is that they change as the environment and markets change. Nonetheless, the broad thinking and direction must extend for a significant period beyond short-term planning cycles. This can often be a shock to newly appointed leaders who, on the way up, have probably had only limited exposure to this high level of strategic thinking.

According to A G Lafley, chairman and chief executive officer of Procter & Gamble in Cincinnati, 'the CEO has a very specific job that only he or she can do: link the external world with the internal organization'.[3] He goes on to say that 'the CEO alone experiences the meaningful outside at an enterprise level and is responsible for understanding it, interpreting it, advocating it, and presenting it so that the company can respond in a way that enables sustainable sales, profit, and total shareholder return growth'.

This suggests that exposure to business strategy, or elements of this, should be given to people before they reach this level and as part of their development. You may recall from the previous chapter that this is a feature of the development that companies such as B-M and GMG offer people whose development plan is moving them towards a leadership role.

Implementing the strategy

While everyone is clear that the top team has the prime responsibility of creating the business strategy, their role in implementing it is often hazy. I have known many instances where there is a discernible disconnect between the people at the top and their direct reports. This generally comes about because senior managers see their role as 'being strategic' and believe that 'being operational' is what their direct reports do. They fail to realize that unless they create a bridge between the two it leaves a gap, with senior management not appreciating what is going on in the rest of the organization and with people below them feeling undirected, unsupported and unclear about what is expected of them. As well as leading to disaffection, this also means that the organization does not follow a clear strategic path but diffuses its effort. People at lower levels take the broad, and probably vague, 'strategy' and interpret the detail so that it may well diverge from what was originally intended. Often the director moves in, late in the day, and others perceive this as moving the goalposts. This does not mean that people at the top should micro-manage. Far from it, but keeping too distant from strategy implementation – which often arises from keeping too distant from actually managing people – does not help create the shared vision and shared understanding required for the new leadership model. Good strategy implementation requires the right balance between being hands on and hands off.

One approach for achieving this balance is to 'lead with questions, not answers'. In *Good to Great*, Jim Collins states that 'great leaders engage in dialogue and debate, not coercion'.[4] This argues for a coaching style of management and against prescriptive micro-management, on the grounds that it demotivates on the one hand but also cuts off innovation, ideas and feedback from lower levels in the business.

The following example from Sergio Marchionne, CEO of Fiat, who is widely credited for having guided Fiat from near bankruptcy to multimillion dollar profits, is also insightful. Marchionne believes it is important to get closely involved but he emphasizes that he is not prescriptive in his style: 'I immerse myself in the business not so that I can make decisions in my corner office but so that I can guide the folks on the ground to make the right decisions. I don't know what those will be, going into a meeting, but I think my involvement makes it more likely that we will get the right ones coming out.'[5]

The prime role of the leader is to ensure that their organization has an appropriate strategy and direction – though it is irrelevant whether leaders actually create it themselves. In fact, an attribute of talent management is that strategic opportunities can be spotted and created by anyone, anywhere. Leaders are the enablers and communicators of vision, values and strategy, a consideration that takes us from the question of how they make it happen to the related one of how they make it change.

There is a marvellous quotation attributed to the economist John Maynard Keynes when he was challenged for having changed his position: 'When the facts change, I change my mind. What do you do?'

Facts do change; markets change; competitors come up with new ideas; technology changes. The need to adapt strategy to such changing circumstances emphasizes the importance of effective communication through the management of people. Writers on strategy emphasize that the insights that lead to competitive advantage emerge not from ivory-tower thinking but from a deep understanding of products, markets and companies' internal processes and capabilities. To achieve this, leaders need either to embody all these capabilities in themselves or else enable their colleagues to input their expertise and insights into the development of new products, services and strategies, to make up for inevitable deficiencies.

This brings us back to the importance of leaders keeping involved in strategy implementation, using debate and influence to create shared vision, values and understanding, but also to ensure strategy is thought through adequately and driven through. To do this, they must constantly pose 'What if' questions, play devil's advocate, test ideas and encourage their subordinates to do the same. This requires regular one-to-one meetings with their direct reports as well as team meetings. In short, it requires good line management, which, at the highest levels, strengthens implementation, motivation and strategic direction. This lays strong foundations for talent management.

Managing the team

From my experience, senior managers often neglect this vital part of their roles, perhaps because the necessity to actively manage direct reports gets lost in the transition to the top team. Their focus shifts to being strategic and outward looking and stepping back from the day to day. This is right, but should not be at the expense of managing direct reports, where I often see a failure on the part of CEOs and directors to have those all-important conversations about performance and careers. At this level, especially, con-versations often focus exclusively on 'hard' business objectives. In the preceding section, I mentioned that people at the top are often too hands off when it comes to strategy implementation. This also translates into being too hands off as line managers, and leads to a disconnection in approach: the opposite of the shared understanding that needs to be achieved.

Perhaps this stepping back from active line management allows too much emotional space that leads top-team members to put their energies into fighting departmental battles. This creates a knock-on effect, often characterized by 'silo working', where information remains in the narrow departmental silo rather than flowing through the organization. Frequently these individuals are not effective as a top team and pass on these wrong behaviours to their own direct reports. Their discussions with them are about hard and impersonal issues, rarely of the meaningful, more personal variety. This is what leads to a disconnection between top management and their departments so that while they set vague directions they are too removed from implementation either to ensure it is effective or to know, in detail, what is going on.

I have mentioned often in this book the importance of team working and collaboration. Teams, however, are made of individuals and individuals do not come together effectively as a team unless they feel they are treated as individuals. The team leader, or in this case the CEO, must achieve the appropriate balance between giving people individual attention and bringing them together as a team to discuss issues openly, and develop team spirit. Included in this is the importance of giving recognition. The Gallup research finding that identifies the importance of recognition as a driver of employee engagement ('In the last seven days, I have received recognition or praise for good work') applies as much to people at the top as to everyone else.[6]

Overall management of vision, values and strategy

I said at the outset of this chapter that these four leadership roles interact, so let us consider them as an overall process, paying particular attention to the last: line managing their direct reports. Figure 9.2 illustrates how information and communication pass back and forth as the business leaders carry out their key roles. Quite separately from their role of recruiting, developing, motivating and deploying their staff they are also communicating in ways set out in Table 9.1.

Think about the communication each leader has with the inside world and specifically with their team. This is both seeking and giving information and giving instructions but, while that is a separate role from, say, developing an individual, it is also indistinguishable from it. The conversation between leader and direct report that results in information passing each way also results in motivation and development of that individual; and through success in the latter process improves the quality of the former. It is also how people achieve a common and shared understanding. For example, the leader chooses to engage in a coaching style of behaviour with an individual in order to enable them to understand an issue for themselves and to be able to deal with similar situations on their own in future. Yet during the same conversation the leader communicates an alteration in strategy and receives back an idea that will subsequently be agreed and will affect the implementation of strategy in the future. You cannot draw precise demarcation lines between the leadership roles and the process of leadership: they are intertwined. It is this process of conversation and transparency that must be transmitted through the organization.

The interactions with the outside world in the realm of implementing strategy comprise a rather different type of communication, since they are primarily physical actions: things the company does and outcomes they observe.

TABLE 9.1 Leadership roles: internal and external

Leadership roles	Inside world	Outside world
Values and vision	Communicating the company ethos and vision to their team and colleagues Receiving ideas, values and data that help to formulate and also feedback that helps to adjust vision and values, from their team and other colleagues	Communicating the company ethos and vision to external stakeholders Receiving ideas, values and data that help to formulate and also feedback that helps to adjust vision and values, from external stakeholders
Creating strategy	Communicating the strategy to team and colleagues Receiving ideas and data that help to formulate and also feedback on issues, problems and outcomes that help to adjust strategy, from their team and other colleagues	Communicating strategy to external stakeholders such as investors and financiers Receiving ideas and data that help to formulate and also feedback on issues, problems and outcomes that help to adjust strategy, from external stakeholders
Implementing strategy	Directions to team Operational information and feedback on outcomes from team and colleagues	Actions to implement strategy Outcomes and responses from the outside world

The breakdown of collaboration

Effective leadership from the top is not only about fulfilling roles; the senior management team also sets the tone, often by how they behave together and how effectively they work as a team. The dysfunctional senior team is a common problem. To paraphrase Tolstoy, every dysfunctional team is dysfunctional in its own way; and yet ... there are commonalities across many different situations. The key breakdown is in the chief executive's role of managing direct reports: usually the rest of the top team. Often it results from the odd idea that once individuals reach the top of an organization they no longer need managing. Of course, this is quite untrue: the necessary style of management may be different but they are still a team and still need managing. Dysfunctionality comes from directors competing for territory and priority, which leads to silo working right through the organization, lack of coordination, wasted effort, low morale and an inability to reach agreement on policy or cooperation to implement it – with a consequent adverse effect on performance. As factions war they each compete for the chief executive's ear and try to avoid bad news. From my experience, as directors split into warring factions this can carry through the organization in a subtle bullying culture, where people's views, input and contribution are often ignored and definitely unrecognized. In terms of Figure 9.2, the information flows are disrupted and it is as if there is a series of vertical splits down the organization, as illustrated in Figure 9.3.

FIGURE 9.3   The breakdown of collaboration

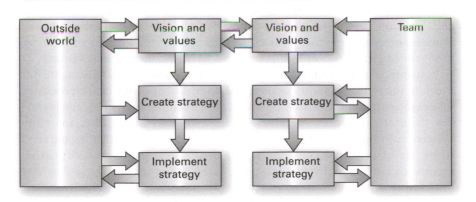

The different functions are not quite completely separate organizations, because they must communicate between and through each other. The marketing department still needs operations to do the manufacturing and still needs information from the sales department but, at each interface, there is a lack of coordination and information flow. As an example, in one organization the purchasing department placed orders for board and packaging four months ahead, yet the sales department's forecasts of demand were done on a three-monthly cycle. The invariable result was a mismatch that led to either excessive stocks being held or an inability to supply customers and therefore lost sales. This was fundamentally a problem of the top team not being managed – nothing else can explain the buyers failing to ask for four-month forecasts or the sales team failing to ask why there was insufficient packaging.

While 'heroic' or 'charismatic' leadership models may no longer be appropriate, this in no way lessens the role of the CEO and the top team. It emphasizes the importance of teamwork at the top. In particular, it places the CEO as the main influencer, line managing direct reports so as to drive employee engagement, build a culture of innovation and collaboration by creating a cohesive top team, mobilizing effort by promoting cultural values, and developing strategy and overseeing its implementation. These are key capabilities that need to start at CEO level.

Leadership of innovation

Figures 9.2 and 9.3 and Table 9.1, by illustrating the interconnectedness of the roles and processes of the organization, also illustrate the importance of collaboration in so much of innovation: a process that, I continually stress, is needed everywhere in today's uncertain business world. What do we mean by innovation? How do people innovate and what encourages innovation?

Sometimes innovation is about a big new idea or a radical insight, but much of the time it is about incremental improvements that make processes more efficient; and often it is somewhere between the two. Hofstede identifies cultural differences in how people champion innovation. In many Western cultures, especially the UK and the USA, he suggests that people need to be free of rules and constraints, and need champions who will provide them with autonomy from rules, procedures and systems so that they can establish creative solutions to existing problems.[7] While Hofstede's work is complex and contains many more permutations than can be described here, it does support the notion that, certainly in the UK and the USA, innovation is more likely to occur in organizational cultures that allow freedom, autonomy and flexibility.

Much of the time, innovation is about people sharing information and knowledge, building on each other's ideas and finding new ways of thinking about old problems. This requires people to work together cooperatively, being prepared to continually review and improve practices and processes. You can never remove competition completely from inside the organization, as people will always compete for jobs and resources, and some competition is healthy. However, as Lynda Gratton describes, 'innovative capacity comes from the intelligence, insights and wisdom of people working together. A combination of individual energy and relational energy generated between them.'[8] Gratton's thesis is that successful organizations are places where people are excited about working together. 'Teams that create a Hot Spot in organizations are energized and buzzing with inspiration. They know that, working together, they will make a difference by achieving something brilliant, important and purposeful, with a strong impact on the bottom line.'

Increasingly, forms of cooperation are becoming more diverse as businesses outsource or enter alliances, partnerships and joint ventures, so that many people in the organization have responsibilities and accountabilities across organizational boundaries. In such cases, you may have no formal authority over people you depend upon to achieve your goals. Additionally, many people work in virtual teams or matrix structures which also require collaborative rather than competitive ways of working. As we set out in Chapter 2, values bind people, they create a corporate identity or brand and they help provide boundaries within which they operate. So in a sense they enable the organization to loosen control and confine rules, systems and procedures to an essential minimum.

GMG's core business, Guardian News and Media (GNM), works hard to maintain its creative edge through collaboration. In 2000, working with GNM on an organization-wide employee engagement survey, we found that staff who work with colleagues in other departments experience a high level of cooperation. GNM consciously encourages cooperation and collaboration through, for example, organizing facilitated programmes that bring people together from across the business to find solutions to specific challenges the company is facing.

Creating a working environment that facilitates collaboration was clearly a guiding principle of the approach that GNM took when planning its office move to a stunning, state-of-the art, purpose-built office block within the new King's Place development in central London. Alison Hall, head of change management at GNM, who was a project manager for the move, explained that when planning the new building, one of the key aims was to 'create a working space that would foster collaboration and integration and bring about a change of how people work and also break down any silos'.

Building the leadership pipeline

Attracting present and future leaders and ensuring a sufficient supply of people coming through is a major challenge for chief executives especially and for all senior managers. Indeed, the 'War for Talent' debate started from the research finding that there were insufficient leaders to go round.

Attracting talent and building the leadership pipeline isn't, as so many think, about management information or control mechanisms (though these are required). It isn't something you can leave to HR and then blame on them if it goes wrong. This is something that the chief executive and senior management team need to see as part of their talent management responsibilities. In spite of the global recession in 2008–9, there is still a shortage of leaders worldwide. As Jim Collins so aptly puts it, 'First who, then do' is of major importance, otherwise business leaders are going to find that they do not have the right people to take the business forward and bring new ideas to fruition.[9]

Marchionne illustrates this approach, seeing 'finding and engaging with new leaders' as a major aspect of his role, and he describes how he spends considerable time engaging with the people coming through the organization: 'I spend four to five months conducting performance reviews for the top 700 people. Of course I look at numbers in assessing performance, but I'm more interested in how well they lead people and lead change. I have long debates with people about whether or not they've displayed the right characteristics. My assessment is based overwhelmingly on this engagement. They know that I care about what happens to them.'[10] Marchionne goes on to say that 'if the organization can feel that kind of connection with its leadership, you're going to get a pretty sound culture aligned around strongly held common values', which also illustrates the point about communicating and managing.

Building the leadership pipeline is the most tangible of the leader's responsibilities for talent management. Where your senior leaders do not readily embrace other aspects of talent management, this can well be the hook to get them involved. I discuss this further in the next chapter.

Building the leadership pipeline is, of course, also one of the most critical requirements of talent management. This is wholly consistent with an inclusive approach, which emphasizes that everyone is important. Growing your own leaders is a necessity for the purposes of business continuity, but also to have the right people to enable the business to take advantage of growth opportunities. Moreover, evidence shows that promoting internal people to senior posts, instead of recruiting externally, has a positive overall impact on retention and motivation.

How can leaders develop the capabilities they require?

Clearly, there is no one-size-fits-all solution but this set of measurement criteria from Stephen Kaufman of the Harvard Business School is useful for focusing senior leaders' minds on areas of development. Kaufman describes

the evaluation process that Arrow Electronics uses to measure the performance of the chief executive:

- Leadership. How well does the CEO motivate and energize the
  organization and is the company's culture reinforcing its mission and
  values?
- Strategy. Is it working, is the company aligned behind it, and is it
  being effectively implemented?
- People management. Is the CEO putting the right people in the right
  jobs, and is there a stream of appropriate people for succession and
  to support growth goals?
- Operating metrics. Are sales, profits, productivity, asset utilization,
  quality, and customer satisfaction heading in the right direction?
- Relationships with external constituencies. How well does the CEO
  engage with the company's customers, suppliers, and other
  stakeholders?[11]

Although this is stated rather differently from my diagram of leadership
roles, it covers the same issues. What Kaufman calls leadership matches my
vision and values: strategy amalgamates creation and implementation; his
view of people management is similar to mine, though possibly understating
the importance of being a line manager to one's team. I am also inclined to
emphasize more strongly leadership accountability for attracting, developing, deploying and engaging talent; the operating metrics role relates to the
implementation of strategy to the outside world and is represented by the
arrows at the bottom left of the diagram; external constituencies are represented by my information flows between the organization and the outside
world.

These measurement criteria are helpful, not only for measuring performance but also for measuring the capability gap for each individual leader to
help them identify their development needs.

Many of the ideas and suggestions throughout this book are relevant to
leaders and board development, including the profiling and development
centre processes discussed in Chapter 7. Coaching is also valuable and one
of the reasons for the explosion in the use of executive coaching in recent
years has been to help people at the top who are leading significant organizational change efforts. The old saying, 'It's lonely at the top', is very true.
The higher your position in the organization, the less likely you are to receive
honest feedback. Greater visibility is accompanied by higher levels of scrutiny.
An executive's decisions become increasingly pivotal and mistakes prove
more costly. An experienced coach fills the gap by providing frank, objective
support and feedback. In the quest for innovation and creativity, a coach can
give the business leader the opportunity to sound out and think through
ideas without inadvertently creating disquiet amongst their team.

Development for emerging leaders must also focus strongly on the specific
technical capabilities of the business, including those identified as important

for the future. Typically, emerging leaders' development will aim to ensure that someone gains appropriate experience, such as international experience or running a small business unit or negotiating at highest government levels, together with formal, structured training, coaching or mentoring.

At GMG, for example, Gray has introduced an emerging leaders programme. This is a high-quality, custom-designed programme, run in conjunction with leading business schools, academics and external practitioners. Its aims and content are geared to the future capabilities foreseen to be critical to the leadership of the business. Importantly, this programme is followed up with opportunities for continuous development. For example, once someone has completed this programme, they are encouraged to become involved in one of the future-focused initiatives going on in the different companies, such as '2020 at GNM', which has people from different parts of the business working together on what the business might look like in 10 years' time.

A business's leaders are the chief influencers of talent management in both word and deed. How they promote vision and values, create and implement strategy, work together and encourage collaboration and innovation, connect directly to talent management. It sets the stage from which you can present talent systems and encourage a mindset that will help the business:

- retain flexibility in an uncertain and unpredictable world;
- be ready to exploit the opportunities of change;
- create business continuity and sustainable futures;
- achieve long-term success and competitive advantage.

My aim in this discussion has been twofold: first, to give a practical understanding of the leader's role to help you put talent management in place. Second, I have sought to give an understanding of the leadership capabilities, which together with the 'new world' behavioural capabilities (problem solving, managing conflict, learning and adapting), you must include in leadership assessment and development programmes.

The following case studies illustrate both of these points within the context of leadership. In the Standard Chartered example we see how leadership effectiveness training and coaching links to the bank's 'strengths finder' model. KPMG has integrated its people processes around the coaching model. Although KPMG does not use the terms 'meaningful conversations' and 'meaningful opportunity', their approach is similar and serves to illustrate these points.

Standard Chartered case study

Year on year, Standard Chartered seeks to further develop and improve its overall employee engagement strategy first started in 2003. As described in an earlier chapter, the guiding principle for this strategy is the bank's philosophy, rooted in positive psychology, of 'strengths-based' management. This is closely linked to one of Standard Chartered's employee engagement survey indicators: 'Every day I have the opportunity to do what I do best.'

The basic premise is that to effectively manage people, the best approach is to focus on enhancing people's strengths rather than try and eliminate their weaknesses. Standard Chartered's aim is, therefore, to provide tools and processes, including an online profiling tool, to make this aim a reality for every employee. In particular, this means encouraging individuals and managers to understand what strengths are, how a role can be tailored to someone's strengths, and how to balance a personal development plan so that someone can build on their strengths. This philosophy permeates all people practices at Standard Chartered.

Geraldine Haley, group head of leadership effectiveness and succession, runs a team of six facilitators who work with over 200 of Standard Chartered's senior leaders and over 50 leadership teams globally.

Each leader has a talent contract that, essentially, sets out a leadership effectiveness development plan for the person, how this will be achieved, within what time frame and with what support. The person's online strengths profile, 360-degree feedback data, performance data and their aspirations are the main inputs used for drawing up this leadership effectiveness plan. Support on following through on this plan is provided by the person's line manager, and if required, interventions from a coach, tutor or a facilitator from Haley's team. For newly appointed leaders or leaders in a new role, there is also a 100-day transition planning programme. Individuals may also draw on Haley and her team for support in developing their teams.

Haley believes that the leadership effectiveness programme brings significant benefits. For example, she says, 'Bankers are often driven by data and results. This has provided them with a different way of doing things that has encouraged them to be better people managers. The strengths-based initiative acts as organizational glue. It gives us a common language and helps create global consistency. If you are a manager or a leader you can go to a Standard Chartered office in a different part of the world and find that some things remain the same. Moreover, we are a networked organization and we fundamentally believe in collaboration and teamwork. This strengths-based approach reinforces this. It isn't threatening – it's recognizing that everyone is different. It encourages diversity and inclusiveness. It's a simple philosophy that has created a more encouraging environment and that engages people more easily.'

Haley also believes that a significant benefit is derived from the fact that they are putting so much resource into the top 250 people. This makes people very conscious that this is what you have to do and how to do it – who you are in the world, what difference you are making. The whole dialogue creates a different philosophy.

Engagement survey and HR information systems data indicate that attrition rates for this group of employees is low compared to benchmark.

Haley also uses the strengths profile in the team development programmes she and her team run on a bespoke basis for senior leadership teams. Sometimes the aim is to help a newly formed team to develop a cohesive team spirit and way of working together; sometimes the aim is to help a team that has run into difficulties. Haley believes passionately that when working with teams, it is important to address the quality of conversations between the leader and team members. These must be open and frank but neither patronizing nor intimidating: people must feel they can put forward ideas without being 'shot down'. A supportive and constructive approach will encourage openness in both directions and improve the quality of ideas. Using a consistent model and a consistent philosophy helps make these conversations non-threatening.

The Standard Chartered programme illustrates the many benefits to be gained from an integrated talent management system. It especially illustrates the advantages of a consistent and cohesive approach in building people's skills, emphasizing the importance of behaviours, and developing the culture of the organization. It is interesting to note the bank's use of a profiling process. Although the tool is different, the application of it to build skills and link processes is similar to the ABC case study, achieving similarly good results. The close connection between Standard Chartered's talent programme and business needs is also noteworthy.

KPMG case study

KPMG is another organization that has achieved consistency and cohesion through an approach that recognizes coaching as one of its strategic levers for change. In evolving coaching, KPMG has aligned its people processes around the key messages that coaching is seeking to reinforce. Its people management leadership is an example. KPMG views taking on people leadership responsibilities as a key role that someone can play in their career. It is one of the best ways to understand how to motivate, retain and develop staff, and this experience really aids individuals when they are looking at entry into partnership, where stewardship and people leadership are key qualities. This is supported by a firm belief in KPMG that it is not just what you do but how you do it. This too reinforces the role of coaching.

These key messages are also embedded in the performance management process. How people manage teams or projects is assessed. KPMG looks at its management style and how individuals bring a team with them to deliver the best result for their clients. KPMG actively looks for evidence that the individual is developing and coaching staff around them to ensure that they are able to deliver on both short- and long-term objectives in a way that fosters team development and learning.

Within KPMG's performance management process, people self-assess on achievement of targets, and also on how effectively they uphold the values of the firm, and they will be asked to produce evidence of this. There is a well-embedded framework in the organization of giving feedback, and people have conversations at the end of any large project to discuss how the work went and any learning that emerges. People also e-mail each other for feedback, generally by asking, 'Can you tell me what to stop, start and continue?' People take this evidence to their appraisal to discuss and reflect on with their performance manager, who takes this into account, together with feedback they have gathered when assessing an individual against KPMG's performance criteria. Overall performance ratings depend on the delivery of consistent results, as well as on demonstrating appropriate behaviours and upholding the firm's values.

KPMG uses a balanced scorecard approach for setting objectives for its partner and director population, having identified what is important for the firm's success. Cascading from these, it has key performance indicators for assessing the impact of its emerging leader population (those deemed to have the potential to reach partner). These work around objectives such as how much someone has depth and breadth in their client portfolio, how international their experience is, how much they have worked across skill sets and how they have added exceptional value to clients.

In establishing more formal coaching, KPMG is introducing a range of different initiatives:

- Developing the capability of its internal coaching faculty, which is unique in that the coaches are full-time professional coaches responsible for coaching delivery and coaching thought leadership within KPMG.
- Boosting the internal coaching faculty by introducing the role of lead coach (a senior 'heavyweight' coach) in each part of the business.
- Encouraging partners to act as mentors, especially to those identified as emerging leaders.
- Rolling out new global training for partners, directors and people management leaders around embedding coaching.
- Formal coaching for new teams that haven't worked together before, so that they can understand team dynamics better.
- Improving selection and contracting with external coaches to achieve greater consistency in terms offered, but also to identify people who are able to coach in a specialist area.

When someone is identified as an emerging leader, they will work with a coach and their sponsoring partner in a consultative way: for example, discussing their 360-degree feedback review and identifying coaching triggers such as points of transition in their careers, taking on new responsibilities, areas they wish to improve. They are also assigned a mentor. Mentors must possess the capabilities required of an emerging leader, as well as understand the value of coaching and mentoring others. The role of the mentor is to provide broader career and internal exposure to the emerging leader, as well as to be someone 'safe' with whom the emerging leader can discuss their concerns and uncertainties. Many mentors are partners, or have themselves been identified as future partners.

On the whole, partners have been keen to take on a mentoring role, seeing it as bringing them added kudos. KPMG has offered guidance on being a mentor but has not introduced formal training. According to Jodie King, KPMG's head of talent management, this is a positive reflection on the culture of KPMG and the mentoring and coaching skills and behaviours that people throughout the organization already have.

In arranging coaching for senior partners, King finds that senior partners usually have a clear idea of why they need a coach, generally requiring a coach who may be sourced internally or externally and who is a cross between a coach and a mentor.

For King, the key to embedding coaching is the very open leadership style in the firm. People at the top will explicitly speak about the benefit they have received from coaching and mentoring in their career and are also quoted in brochures or other literature on this.

King believes there is considerable evidence to show that KPMG offers a full and rewarding career. King's own role has been built around the recognized need that the firm must do more to build the capability of its future leaders, and investment has been prioritized here and formalized into an emerging leaders programme. In building this capability, emphasis has been placed on the importance of managers having open and honest conversations with staff about their performance and careers, and KPMG has put a great deal of investment into supporting line managers to have these conversations, for example through training, coaching and mentoring and support for their people management leaders.

This case study illustrates the importance of a consistent and integrated approach, where processes and interventions are built around important concepts that in themselves are critical not only to achieve talent management but also to business performance. In KPMG's case, this is to establish an approach that affects how people relate to one another internally, but crucially also transfers to the quality of their client relationships. As KPMG has for many years appeared at or near the top of The Sunday Times Best Companies to Work For survey, this demonstrates the success of its approach.

These two case studies illustrate many characteristics of talent management raised throughout this book, especially the importance of a consistent and integrated approach that focuses on equipping managers with the skills of holding important conversations about performance and careers. They illustrate also the importance of continuing with an approach and aligning it with the visions, values and strategies of the business.

LEARNING POINTS

- The CEO and senior management are the chief influencers of talent management in both word and deed.

- Their four leadership roles in talent management are: to espouse and promote vision and values; to create strategy; to implement the strategy; and to manage their team.

- Leaders set the tone and direction of the business and must encourage a climate of collaboration that fosters innovation.

- Leaders must have clear accountability for building the leadership pipeline and growing people from within.

References

1 Kouzes, J M and Posner, B Z (2009) To lead, create a shared vision, *Harvard Business Review*, January

2 Wasserman, N (2009) Planning a start-up? Seize the day, *Harvard Business Review*, January

3 Lafley, A G (2009) What only the CEO can do, *Harvard Business Review*, January

4 Collins, J (2001) Good to Great, *Fast Company*, October

5 Marchionne, S (2008) Fiat's extreme makeover, *Harvard Business Review*, December

6 Harter, J K *et al* (2006) Gallup Q12 Meta-Analysis

7 Hofstede, G (2001) *Culture's Consequences: comparing values, behaviors, institutions, and organizations across nations*, 2nd edn, Sage Publications

8 Gratton, L (2007) *Hot Spots: why some companies buzz with energy and innovation – and others don't*, Pearson Education, Harlow

9 Jim Collins speaking at CIPD's Annual Conference and Exhibition, Manchester 2009

10 Marchionne, S (2008) Fiat's extreme makeover, *Harvard Business Review*, December

11 Kaufman, S P (2008) Evaluating the CEO, *Harvard Business Review*, October

The role of HR: Gaining acceptance to talent management

In this chapter I put forward ways to help HR gain acceptance for the ideas discussed in this book. I also show examples from the experiences of leading HR practitioners and draw guidance from these.

Ideally, a talent management strategy requires the support and commitment of the people at the top. Evidence suggests that senior management are increasingly recognizing the link between people and business performance. For example, ACE International HR Barometer found that in 56 per cent of organizations, 'HR is included proactively in top-level strategic planning'.[1] This figure rises to 62 per cent in the UK. Nonetheless, that still leaves many organizations where the top team may not be on board with what you are trying to achieve. Moreover, an intellectual appreciation of it is not the same as having a practical understanding. There is often a gap at senior levels between knowing and doing.

If you have active support from the top, then introduce your talent strategy, as set out in this book, by getting the people at the top involved in setting the vision, values and strategic direction, and then gradually introduce the rest of your strategy.

If you do not have this support, it is still important to draw up a talent strategy, as this will ensure you connect activities and transmit consistent messages. Think of it as a jigsaw puzzle. Putting the first pieces together is hardest. It's difficult to work out how it all fits together, and you are not sure where it is all leading. As the jigsaw starts to come together, it gets easier to fill in the remaining pieces. The whole picture starts to build up in your mind, and by the time you get to the last few pieces, you are on a roll. The whole jigsaw must, however, be designed first, and then broken up. You cannot design a jigsaw the other way around. It is the same with talent management. Without a strategy, you are less likely to offer people a coherent way of doing things that fits together, and you lose the opportunity to build pictures in people's minds.

Generate insights

David Reay, who has held both HR business partner and corporate HQ roles, believes it is vital that HR 'regularly spends time having one-to-one conversations with directors about what is happening and the challenges they face. Most of the insights are in their heads, and HR can play an important role in surfacing these insights and translating them into new ways of doing things.'

David Fairhurst of McDonald's also emphasizes the value of conversations and insight: 'Few people have the insight that is required to monitor the needs of people in the future. You must ask: what is evolving, changing, driving the business? Identify the operational income drivers for the next five years and then identify the capability gap on any one of those drivers. Look at the shifts and what's changed. This might throw up a whole new set of capabilities. talent management is not about filling shoes.'

Paul Herrick of Burson-Marsteller defines talent as matching job opportunities with people's aspirations. He believes a leader should want to find out about everyone: what motivates them, what their dreams and preferences are, what they want to do, and what their capabilities and potential are. His views inspire the firm's innovative approach to global development, with its emphasis on meeting people's aspirations, and on providing them with opportunity and development. This has talent management and the HR function at the very centre of leading-edge businesses.

Pull levers

Next, identify an immediate priority that is concerning your senior team, and use this as a lever to introduce the part of your talent strategy that will best help. Reay, for example, finds that 'business continuity is a major concern at the top brought about for a whole host of reasons, such as sustainability issues, and increasing emphasis on risk awareness. A succession plan that puts people in boxes and then goes into a drawer leaves the organization vulnerable, especially at times of rapid change, skills shortages and recruitment difficulties. Leverage this to introduce dynamic processes and an emphasis on development.'

For many businesses, shortages of people to fill key roles lead to lack of business agility to meet new challenges. This is a lever for a dynamic succession planning process that includes talent review conversations. Purshouse of Bekaert believes 'this goes full circle. Top-level talent reviews raise awareness and lead to a better understanding of what HR can do. This in turn makes senior and other line managers more aware of their talent management responsibilities and of where and why they need support.'

Generally, senior managers are focused on the future and can be persuaded by an approach that is, essentially, about future proofing the organization and achieving long-term success and sustainability. The promise of a better future is, however, less likely to win over line managers caught up in the here and now. This means that HR must seek to understand the pressures they face and craft solutions that do not just provide a quick fix but are consistent with the overall talent strategy.

Sometimes there is an obvious problem that offers an opportunity to act as a channel for change, such as a star performer leaving, high staff turnover or high absence levels. One department head of an advertising agency found her clients regularly requested staff turnover and diversity information to be included in proposals, which led her to approach HR for support. The HR business partner of an accountancy firm understood the pressures the firm's accountants were facing from clients and promoted coaching skills, using the argument that they are transferable between client- and staff-facing roles. In a manufacturing concern, the HR manager realized that a planned change in manufacturing processes to meet a new business stream would demand different project management skills from people and introduced this as a proactive measure.

Sometimes the pressure comes from staff. The European Southern Observatory (ESO) in Germany is an intergovernmental organization whose remit includes building and operating a suite of the world's most powerful ground-based astronomical telescopes. ESO has been based in Garching, near Munich, since 1980. The culture of the organization and its management processes had largely evolved to meet the needs of its scientists and astronomers, many of whom are long-serving employees who are highly engaged with their work and have a clear sense of purpose. Recently, Sam Austin-May, ESO's deputy head of HR, recognized that the organization had reached a point where a step change was necessary. Demand was coming particularly from new recruits and technical/scientific staff across all disciplines who wanted different things: more development opportunity, feedback, recognition and involvement. Austin-May listened to the problems staff were experiencing. She used these as a lever to engage line managers in a management development programme that would equip them to make this step change, but that would also generate a cohesive and coherent management culture. The programme has made considerable impact and Austin-May is now finding that people are demanding more.

The point here is that good HR leads to more HR.

As I have emphasized before, however, it is not the systems that are important but how you use them.

Create a talent mindset

One of our aims with talent management is to create a talent mindset where conversations and judgement take precedence over following procedures. This does not denigrate systems; but they must facilitate these conversations and enable this judgement to develop.

A talent mindset:

- manages people for their strengths and preferences;
- recognizes the importance of understanding people's aspirations and of providing them with meaningful opportunity to help them meet these;
- actively plans for future capability requirements;
- matches people to roles through an understanding of the capabilities they possess, not by virtue of their experience alone;
- recognizes the importance of regularly conducting meaningful conversations about performance and careers.

Most HR systems and processes were developed for the purposes of control but this results in many unintended consequences: performance appraisal formalities that line managers find a nightmare, 360-degree feedback and succession plans that end up filed in the bottom drawer, people notified of pay awards through their payslips, people whose poor performance brings down standards and places undue pressure on their colleagues. Organizations are left to languish, or worse, while it takes months to appoint a successor to the chief executive. People who want a change of direction or fresh challenge seek opportunities outside the organization because it is easier and sometimes less humiliating than applying internally. People who have made significant contributions are required to reapply for their jobs, or re-tender in the name of 'fair' competition. I could go on. But in the 'new world', it is time to reassess all our processes, minimize the control elements and instead focus these processes so that they help line managers have conversations and exercise judgement. Let me give you an analogy from the motor industry. It may seem odd at first, but think about it.

In the beginning there were many craft manufacturers who produced cars at high prices and low quality. Then along came Ford, followed by Sloan at General Motors, who introduced mass production that dramatically reduced prices and improved quality somewhat. But mass production also deskilled processes and led to alienation and industrial relations problems. Then along came lean production, which built on ideas originating in America; it was pioneered in Japan partly because of a cultural resistance there to the alienation aspects of mass production but also because of a recognition, in a more collaborative culture, of the inefficiencies and quality problems of mass production. Lean production reintroduced individual skills and teamwork and commitment and, above all, personal responsibility to the concept of mass production. And, far from being a retrograde move, it reduced costs further, improved quality further and increased the ability of companies to innovate.

Talent management is the lean production of HR processes. It builds on but corrects the old orthodoxy that deskills, depersonalizes and alienates, and it addresses the unintended consequences of a mass-production approach to the management of people. Instead it builds on collaboration, teamwork, personal development and, of course, meaningful conversations between line managers and their staff.

The crucial message here is to use as your basic rule of thumb the question, 'How will this help line managers?' Examine all your processes and systems from this angle, and only implement new ones with this in mind. Talent management is complex to design and involves many component parts, but the effects of it should be to create simplicity and clarity for line managers. It achieves this through consistency and by constantly reinforcing the message.

Can HR leapfrog to talent management?

I believe you can leapfrog to talent management, but as the next case study illustrates, only if you have the basics in place.

ConvaTec case study

Gwynne Hamlen is the vice-president of HR, EMEA, for ConvaTec, a company that develops innovative medical technologies in the fields of wound care, ostomy care, and continence and critical care. Previously part of Bristol-Myers Squibb, a leading player in biopharmaceuticals, ConvaTec became a stand-alone company when it was sold to private equity investors. Previously, ConvaTec had been just one division of a huge multinational on which it relied for most of its HR services, but from 1 August 2008, Hamlen and a small team of UK-based HR generalists had to provide a full HR service for 4,000 employees across much of Europe. These services extended from setting up payroll and benefits plans through to supporting general managers in each country to establish an HR infrastructure encompassing recruitment processes, employee contracts and HR policies, dealing with works councils, and so on. Then, a month later, they had to extend these services to absorb a newly acquired business, Unomedical.

Once these basics were in place, they then implemented a global human resource information system that has enabled them to establish common processes across the world. To set this up, they identified all core processes that exist in an employment life cycle and mapped each one, identifying clearly at each stage the line manager's role and the HR role. In doing this, they worked to a philosophy of HR minimizing its intervention by creating clear guidelines and setting flexible boundaries that empower line managers to manage their people independently and give them freedom to operate and take their own decisions without needing approvals, bureaucracy or HR 'policing'. Headcount is one example of a process HR might previously have 'policed' by requiring approval and justification. Now line managers have clear boundaries to work within and need only make a business case if they wish to go outside them.

The processes Hamlen and her colleagues have established provide corporate consistency and central control but give local offices discretion on implementation. When recruiting, for example, the process sets out that the line manager and immediate superior must interview at some stage in the process, but otherwise local offices use recruitment and selection methods and sources that suit local practices.

The approach that Hamlen, her HR peers and her boss, the senior vice-president of HR, based in the USA, took to establish these employment life cycle processes was part of their broader philosophy of keeping a lean HR function, focusing efforts where these added most value to the business. Hamlen's experience supports the view that it is critical to get the operational aspects of HR in place and working efficiently before attempting to take on a strategic, transformational role. 'There's a load of HR stuff that needs to be done, even though it doesn't add value. The business doesn't care how we run the pension scheme, just that it's there.' Having the foundations in place has also been essential to enable ConvaTec to expand; it means the business can easily slot new people into its infrastructure. To use the analogy of a computer game, having mastered this foundation level, it's now on to the next.

Having put the foundation in place, ConvaTec is now planning to outsource much of it, so that HR can concentrate on its business partner role. Hamlen sees this as 'not being about working with line managers on everything, but just on those critical issues that will really add value. It is about driving business and individual performance and getting the metrics behind it.' She believes strongly that 'the credibility of HR is founded on getting the transactional right. Only when you have done that can you then focus on the transformational.'

Contrast this case study with the example of the newly recruited HR director whose colleagues told him the HR department was ineffective. If he'd delved into this, he would have discovered that the perceived problems were around the day-to-day issues of pay, disciplinary matters and recruitment. Value-added talent management and learning and development initiatives, on the other hand, were well regarded. The point here is that if transactional HR does not run smoothly, it is harder to get recognition for your value-added achievements. In this case, the new HR director threw everything out and introduced a whole range of new initiatives. This wasted considerable investment, but it also meant the real problems went unresolved; and so it goes it on.

Building bridges across HR

In larger HR departments, where responsibilities are more fragmented, building bridges is vital. Jenny Arwas, HR director for BT's HQ functions, illustrates this through her analysis of the journey BT has undertaken over the past 20 years to drastically reduce and transform its HR function.

Arwas has been a driving force behind much of this transformation, which has seen HR move from the role of policeman to that of business partner whose key function is to drive the capability of line managers. To get to this point, the business has outsourced and set up a self-service centre. While this works well in many respects, it is not without its drawbacks and pitfalls. For example, it is a common problem echoed by others in a similar position to Arwas that it is easy for an outsourced service centre to end up acting in a vacuum, somewhat divorced from the business. This prevents those in the transactional roles from learning from those in the transformational roles, and vice versa. For instance, do service centre employees who process appraisal forms pick up from the way they are completed that people's interpretations of competencies differ wildly, suggesting they do not understand them, and do they feed this information back to the HR business partners?

Arwas cites a service centre employee speaking on the telephone from a comfortable, dry and warm call centre in India with a line manager in the north of England who has a problem with an employee who spends a large part of his day in a dark, wet hole, deep underground, and close to cables and sewers. Is the service centre employee really able to empathize and provide good advice to this line manager? Does the service centre employee pick up from calls of this kind what problems and issues are starting to arise in the business? Do they pass this kind of information on to the HR business partners?

Arwas believes that there are great benefits to be gained from working seamlessly with outsourced service centre partners so that both sides can learn from each other and contribute to strategic planning and development, as well as to achieving operational improvements. 'It is all about how you make the model work so that you create an interface between the operational and strategic, so that you can leverage from each other and input reciprocally.'

A lesson here is that it is essential to build bridges across all HR functions if you are to achieve the consistency and cohesion that talent management requires.

In summary, talent management is not a method of calculating how much a few people are worth to the business. It is a way of managing people and leading them to achieve the long-term success of the business.

Reference

1 *ACE International HR Barometer* (2009) www.network-ace.com

APPENDIX A
Mind the gap

Questions about the business environment:

- What changes do you see on the horizon (three, five, 10 years)?
- Competitors, new products, new channels, new technologies, regulation, etc?
- What threats do these pose to you?
- What opportunities do these pose?

Questions specific to the business as a whole:

- What is the business aiming to achieve?
- What will success look like?
- What might prevent this being achieved?
- What might help you achieve this?
- What is driving this change/idea?
- What might hinder it?
- What are your competitors doing?
- What are the variables?
- What are the current strengths of the business?
- What are the gaps?
- What are the milestones?
- What are the current operational income drivers? What's changing?
- What operational income drivers are projected over the next five years?
- What are the key sustainability issues for your organization?
- How might these affect your business plans?
- What will you need to do differently as a result?
- What opportunities might this offer?

Questions specific to the business strategy:

- On what strategic assumptions about the future does your strategy depend?
- Which of these assumptions is the most uncertain?

- What impact would it have on your strategy if these assumptions turn out differently?
- What are the 'what ifs'?
- What are the different assumptions among the top team?
- What talent issues have the biggest impact on budget?
- Who are the most important new hires? Why?
- Where do you need to hire people who are significantly different in order to meet future business plans?
- In what jobs would turnover be a significant problem? Why?

Questions specific to line managers and/or to different business units:

- What are your future business plans over the next two years, five years, 10 years?
- On what strategic assumptions are these plans based?
- What might help them be achieved?
- What are the obstacles?
- What demands will this place on people?
- What technical/behavioural capabilities will these require?
- What are the strengths of the organization?
- Where are the gaps?
- What will people get excited about?
- What risks will be required?
- What does the new strategy require in terms of skills and capabilities in the short term?
- And in the long term?
- Where do these reside at present?
- What are the relatively stable and predictable requirements of this strategy?
- What are the unpredictable requirements of this strategy?
- Which decisions have long-term implications and what are they?

Capabilities required:

- Which roles are critical to enabling you to achieve this strategy?
- What will people have to do differently and how will that be achieved?
- What capabilities will be required for this and objectives/changes?
- Which are certain, which possible?
- What development will be required?
- What are the capability gaps? How are they changing?

- How can these be plugged?
- Which skills are in short supply?
- Where are the roles that need complex skills requiring long training periods?
- Do you invest differentially in critical skills?
- Where does your strategy require talent and organization to be better than those of your competitors to work?
- Where should you pay more and/or spend more?
- What defines critical jobs?
- Which employees make the biggest difference?
- What makes this difference (performance, behavioural capabilities, knowledge, potential)?
- What is the connection between performance differences and business outcomes?
- Where would more people and/or higher performance levels have the greatest effect?
- How will success depend on individual capability, opportunity or motivation?

Implications for achieving capabilities:

- Do we need to recruit or are there individuals able to provide those capabilities?
- What development will they need?
- Will that take them where they want to go?
- Who will be developed to replace them?
- Who will succeed people who currently have key capabilities in two or three years?
- Who has scarce skills and to whom can they pass them and how?
- What are the key milestones in preserving and acquiring capabilities?

FIGURE 11.1   Mind the gap

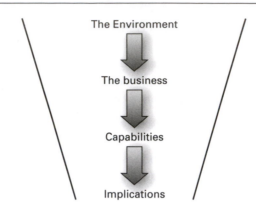

APPENDIX B
Talent management flowchart

FIGURE 11.2   Talent management flowchart

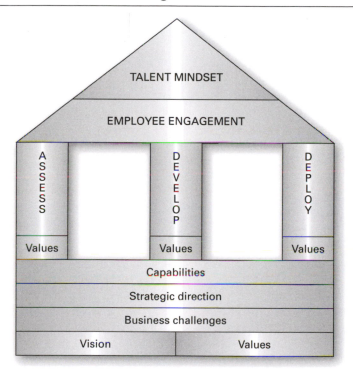

APPENDIX C
Planning talent management

Programme elements	Business	Line manager	Individual
Assess	What capabilities will the business need in the foreseeable future?	Do managers regularly reassess long-term goals and capabilities?	Do people have tools and opportunities to help them diagnose their own strengths and preferences, as well as make development plans?
	How well do we track and review people so that we know what capabilities exist and where?	Do they identify and give feedback to high performers, and to people who make vital but steady contributions?	
	Do we track and review people to maintain high performance levels?	Do they identify poor performers or people performing at the margin?	
	Do we track and review people to ensure people 'live' our espoused values and employer brand?		
	Do we plan for succession and for scarce skills?		
	Do we achieve consistency between internal and external recruitment criteria? Do these cover organizational values and capabilities?		
	Are our reward and recognition programmes aligned to organizational values and capabilities?		
	Do we hold line managers accountable for talent management?		

Programme elements	Business	Line manager	Individual
Develop	Do we provide adequate opportunities for people to develop towards long-term as well as short-term needs (three-stage development plan)?	Do they support and challenge people so that they develop their capabilities and experience? Do they understand people's longer-term aspirations? Do they provide stretching and enriching job opportunities that move people towards their longer-term aspirations?	Do people take advantage of development opportunities provided? Do people seek to learn from their experiences? Do they continually learn to keep up with change? Do people support one another's development?
Deploy	Do we have adequate processes that would enable us to deploy the right people when emerging opportunities arise, quickly and without significant disruption to other parts of the organization? Do people move across organizational boundaries?	Do they enable people to do what they do best every day?[1] Do they encourage and support people to take on different roles and move to different departments?	Do people spot and create new business opportunities?
Engage	Do we give recognition to high performers and those who make a significant contribution? Does everyone understand the organization's plans and achievements and how they fit into these? Is everyone clear about how they contribute to the whole?	Do they hold regular meaningful conversations with staff individually and as a team to answer: How am I doing? How are we doing? What does the future hold? How will I/we get there? How will I/we be rewarded? How are we doing as a team?	Do people take personal responsibility for their own development? Do they collaborate with others, sharing opportunities and information and supporting others' learning?

http://www.gallup.com/consulting/52/employee-engagement.aspx

BIBLIOGRAPHY

The following books, reports, surveys and articles have helped me immensely in writing this book and I strongly recommend them to anyone who wishes to further their understanding of this fascinating subject.

Please note that this is not an exhaustive list of all the references I have used in this book, which are provided at the end of each chapter.

Books

Boudreau, J W and Ramstad, P M (2007) *Beyond HR: the New Science of Human Capital*, Harvard Business School Press, Boston, Mass

Caplan, J (2003) Coaching for the Future: How smart companies use coaching and mentoring, CIPD

Cheese, P, Thomas, R and Craig, E (2008) *The Talent-powered Organization*, Kogan Page, London

Collins, J (2001) *Good to Great: Why Some Companies Make the Leap ... and Others Don't*, Random House

Fincham, R and Rhodes, P (2005) *Principles of Organizational Behaviour*, 4th edn, Oxford University Press, Oxford

Gratton, L (2007) *Hot Spots: why some companies buzz with energy and innovation – and others don't*, Pearson Education, Harlow

Harvard Business Review on Talent Management (2008) Harvard Business Press, Boston, Mass

Hofstede, G (2001) *Culture's Consequences: comparing values, behaviors, institutions, and organizations across nations*, 2nd edn, Sage Publications

Michaels, E, Handfield-Jones, H and Axelrod, B (1997) *The War for Talent*, Harvard Business School Press, Boston, Mass

Roberts, G (1999) Recruitment and Selection: a competency approach, CIPD, London

Sloman, M (2007) *The Changing World of the Trainer: emerging good practice*, Butterworth-Heinemann

Journal articles

Campbell, A and Alexander, M (1997) What's wrong with strategy?, *Harvard Business Review*, November

Lafley, A G (2009) What only the CEO can do, *Harvard Business Review*, January

Kaufman, S P (2008) Evaluating the CEO, *Harvard Business Review*, October

Kouzes, J M and Posner, B Z (2009) To lead, create a shared vision, *Harvard Business Review*, January

Porter, M (1996) What is strategy?, *Harvard Business Review*, November–December
Wasserman, N (2009) Planning a start-up? Seize the day, *Harvard Business Review*, January

Reports, surveys, podcasts

Hirsch, W (2009) *Talent management: practical issues in implementation*, Institute of Employment Studies, UK
Hamel, G (2009) *Building leadership capability for change*, podcast episode 32, www.cipd.co.uk
Purcell, J *et al* (2003) *Understanding the People and Performance Link: Unlocking the Black Box*, CIPD, London
CIPD (2009) *Taking the Temperature of Coaching*, Coaching survey, CIPD, London
Frank Bresser Consulting (2009) *Global coaching survey, executive summary*: http://www.frank-bresser-consulting.com/globalcoachingsurvey09-executivesummary.pdf
Hirsh, W (2000) *Succession planning demystified*, Report 372, Institute for Employment Studies, October
Reilly, P and Brown, D (2008) Employee engagement: what is the relationship with reward management?, *World at Work*, 4th quarter

INDEX

NB: page numbers in *italic* indicate figures or tables

The sharpest minds need the finest advice. **Kogan Page** creates success.

www.koganpage.com

KoganPage

With over 1,000 titles in printed and digital format, **Kogan Page** offers affordable, sound business advice

www.koganpage.com

Kogan Page